The Gift of God:
THE HOLY SPIRIT

ANDREW APOSTOLI, CFR

Preface by Benedict J. Groeschel, CFR

ALBA·HOUSE   NEW·YORK

SOCIETY OF ST. PAUL, 2187 VICTORY BLVD., STATEN ISLAND, NEW YORK 10314

231.3
A645

Library of Congress Cataloging-in-Publication Data

Apostoli, Andrew.
   The gift of God: the Holy Spirit / Andrew Apostoli; preface by
Benedict J. Groeschel.
      p.   cm.
   ISBN 0-8189-0703-7
   1. Holy Spirit.   I. Title.
BT121.2.A66   1994
231'.3 — dc20   94-4450
                                                 CIP

Produced and designed in the United States of America by the
Fathers and Brothers of the Society of St. Paul,
2187 Victory Boulevard, Staten Island, New York 10314,
as part of their communications apostolate.

ISBN: 0-8189-0703-7

Printing Information:

Current Printing - first digit   1   2   3   4   5   6   7   8   9   10

Year of Current Printing - first year shown

| 1994 | 1995 | 1996 | 1997 | 1998 | 1999 |

Dedication

With love and filial piety, this book
is dedicated to Our Blessed Lady who, chosen by
the Father, received the Eternal Word within her womb
and gave Him flesh, by her humble faith and ready
obedience to accept the overshadowing of
the Holy Spirit at the Annunciation!

May her prayers and example assist
all Christians to receive an abundant outpouring
of the Gift of God, the Holy Spirit,
in their personal lives!

Acknowledgments

THIS BOOK WAS BROUGHT to completion with the generous help of a number of persons. Three individuals stand out in a special way: Mary Majkowski, who faithfully typed the text through various revisions (with the assistance of a patient and understanding family who often shared their dinner table with the author!); Rene Bumb, who enthusiastically volunteered her skills editing the text; and my confrere, Father Benedict Groeschel, CFR, who wrote the Preface of the book and made numerous valuable suggestions.

Others who helped in various ways include Camille La Manda, Penny Wolfe, Tara Blackwell, Mary Battersby, Marty Fay, Susan Brawley and Michael Apostoli, the author's brother. Recognition is made of those who offered assistance and encouragement as the project developed, especially that of supportive prayer.

The author wishes to thank Alba House for graciously agreeing to publish this work.

No acknowledgment would be complete without thanking God, from Whom all blessings flow. May this book redound to the glory and praise of the Most Holy Trinity! Gratitude goes to Our Lady, to St. Therese of Lisieux, and the Servants of God, Padre Pio of Pietrelcina, OFM Cap., and Father Solanus Casey, OFM Cap., whose intercession was daily sought throughout the preparation of these pages.

Contents

Preface

R EFERENCES TO THE HOLY SPIRIT, or the Spirit of God, are more common in the last two decades than they were for several centuries. Groups as sharply diverse as the Charismatic Movement and the enthusiasts of the so-called New Age, as well as many others who use the name of the Holy Spirit, will attribute all kinds of effects to this Divine Person. Traditional theologians and feminist writers will evoke the Holy Spirit, attributing gender to a pure Spirit who is neither Father nor Son, thus involving this most mysterious Person in controversies unthought of at the time of the writing of Sacred Scripture. Christians as different as cloistered nuns and Quakers rely heavily on this mysterious influence to direct their prayers and even their lives.

It is startling that with all this interest and activity the scriptural and traditional teaching of the Church on the Holy Spirit is almost unknown. One might ask why the Church has any special claim to tell the world about the Holy Spirit. The fact is that, drawing from the Holy Scriptures and especially from the words of Christ in the Gospels, the bishops of the early Catholic Church gave us the knowledge of the Holy Spirit beginning with the post-apostolic times and coming to a great conclusion at the First Council of Constantinople in 381. Then the Holy Spirit was declared to be a Person and not merely an aspect of divine activity as might appear in the Old Testament. The Holy Spirit is distinct from the Father and the Son. In defining the Holy Spirit as a Person, which means an ultimate subject of predication (e.g., the Holy Spirit does this or that), the bishops of the ancient Church proclaimed the dogma of the Holy Trinity and with it taught that the Holy Spirit can be invoked and responds and has a unique role in the salvation of the world. Since Constantinople I, a rich teaching, both theological and spiritual, both speculative and practical, has developed around the Third Person of the Trinity. But, as I said, very few believers are actually aware of this teaching. My confrere and dear friend, Fr. Andrew Apostoli, has filled this need by writing a readable and down-to-earth book on the Holy Spirit. This book, like all Fr. Andrew's works, is meant for the informed and devout reader. It is both simple and profound, serious and humorous at the same time.

When we began our reform movement, the Franciscans of the Renewal, in 1987, the eight original friars agreed that we had only two apostolates — care of the very poor and evangelical preaching. The Holy Spirit, the Spirit of God, is an essential part of that endeavor. Those familiar with Fr. Andrew's approach and charming humor will hear him as they read these pages. Those who are not familiar with his style and presentations, as well as his deep faith, will admire all of these qualities for the first time. All will find a Spirit-filled fervor, the essential human ingredient for Christian reform.

We are all encouraged in the contemporary Church to pray to the Holy Spirit and to ponder the influence of the Third Person of the Blessed Trinity in our lives with grateful praise. We are encouraged to rely upon the Holy Spirit in times of need and special stress. We are even told that by the gifts of the Holy Spirit we may go beyond our ordinary strength and even beyond the practice of the virtues given us by divine grace. The Holy Spirit can make the timid brave and the foolish wise. He can cause sinners to repent and move the lukewarm to fervor. Thus the Holy Spirit is an important part of the life of every devout Christian. I can't think of any other recent book of this size and popularity that can inform and encourage the believing reader in the practice of Christian life with the help of the Holy Spirit. One hopes that this book will begin a series of books by Fr. Andrew which will make his deep and genuine piety and ability known to a wider audience.

Fr. Benedict J. Groeschel, CFR

Author's Preface

F OR SOME TIME NOW, I have felt a strong desire to write a book on the Holy Spirit. In fact, I hope it will be only the first in a series of books dealing with the Third Person of the Blessed Trinity. What moves me to write is the awareness of how important it is that everyone who follows Jesus and wishes to serve Him and His Church faithfully, should come to know the Holy Spirit personally. Our Lord Himself stressed this importance when He promised to send the Holy Spirit as the Paraclete, guiding, strengthening and consoling all who would follow Him on life's pilgrimage of faith. The early Christians, as reflected in the pages of the Acts of the Apostles, were very conscious of the Holy Spirit living and working among them. St. Paul, witnessing to life in the early Church, could write to the Christians at Rome: "Those who are led by the Spirit of God are children of God" (Romans 8:14).

Despite this undeniable importance, many Catholics still do not know the Holy Spirit. (Some of the causes for this problem will be dealt with in the opening chapter.) It was to share some reflections on the all-important presence and role of the Holy Spirit that this book has been written.

The roots of this book actually go back many years in my life. As a youngster, I remember hearing the Holy Spirit referred to as the "Forgotten God." We pray often to the Father and to the Son, but except for perhaps occasional help on an exam, the Holy Spirit is generally forgotten. I would later hear the expression about the Forgotten God many other times.

This lack of understanding of the Holy Spirit was brought

home to me again very vividly at the time of my priestly ordination. I was ordained on March 16, 1967, in St. Francis de Sales Church in Geneva, New York by Bishop Fulton J. Sheen, then Bishop of the Diocese of Rochester, New York. As a young boy, I used to watch his TV program, "Life is Worth Living," along with probably thirty million other people! Little did I think I would some day meet him, much less ever be ordained by him. He truly loved the Priesthood, and he inspired in me a share of that love! He spoke to me that day about the vital link between the awareness of the Holy Spirit and the faithful, fruitful living of the priestly life. He said that the newly ordained priest receives the special power of the Holy Spirit, through Whom he carries out his priestly vocation. However, he lamented the fact that during my four years of theological training, no significant study was offered on the Holy Spirit. As he saw it, this was a major omission, resulting in a serious lack of understanding for a newly ordained priest. Bishop Sheen's statement made a lasting impression on me. I also realized that if this was my situation as a priest, how much more widespread must be the lack of understanding about the Holy Spirit among the laity!

My desire, then, is to write about the Holy Spirit in such a way that a broad Catholic readership would find it understandable. I have, therefore, made a deliberate effort to avoid, as far as I could, any technical theological language or obscure dogmatic points. There has also been a determined attempt to present this writing in such a manner that readers will not be left dry and unaffected, but rather be touched by the life and unction of the Holy Spirit!

Finally, it is further my hope that this book will be beneficial not only to lay people in general, but that it will appeal to clergy, religious, and seminarians as well. It can have particular value for persons in religious study groups and prayer groups as well as for spiritual direction and personal reading. It can be especially helpful as supplemental reading for use in "Life in the Spirit" seminars.

I give thanks to the Holy Spirit for the enlightenment and perseverance He has given me in writing this book. I assure each reader a place in my prayers, and I ask a prayerful remembrance in return.

Fr. Andrew Apostoli, CFR
St. Felix Friary, Yonkers, New York

I.

THE HOLY SPIRIT: THE GIFT OF GOD

Chapter 1

The Gift of God

W HEN SOMEONE OFFERS another person a gift, the first thing the receiver should do is acknowledge the gift, then express gratitude for it, and finally, put it to good use. This is especially true if God is the Giver of the gift and we are the receivers. God does, in fact, give us many gifts and blessings every day. Everything we are, everything we have, is ultimately a gift from Him.

THE "FORGOTTEN GOD"

One of God's greatest gifts to us is one He Himself calls "the Gift of God" (John 4:10). It is a reference to the Holy Spirit, Whom He in His great love has bestowed so generously upon us! One would think that because we have received such a priceless Gift from God, we would esteem and treasure it above all His other gifts — acknowledging it, expressing gratitude for it, and using it as God intended us to! Yet, the sad fact is that God's most precious Gift to us, the Holy Spirit, is often not acknowledged; indeed, He is often unknown. He has for this reason so frequently been referred to as the "Forgotten God" among the Three Divine Persons of the Blessed Trinity!

The assumption underlying this book is that many Christians, especially many Catholics, do not know and love the Holy Spirit as they should in their personal lives. But this is not a new situation by any means. It is reflected right in the Sacred Scriptures, and it has been recognized over the Church's long history even from its earliest centuries. A few examples will illustrate this clear

Examples From the New Testament

This problem is very clearly presented at least twice in the pages of the New Testament. Let us look briefly at these examples.

The Samaritan woman

The first instance is Jesus' conversation with the Samaritan woman at the well (John 4:4-42). In this incident, the woman has come to draw water from the common well for the day's cooking and cleaning. When the Lord looks at her, He knows the sinful condition of her life, as He Himself will later point out to her:

> You have had five (husbands), and the man you are living with now is not your husband! (John 4:18)

However, Jesus is the Good Shepherd seeking one of His lost sheep. He is the Divine Physician wanting to heal one of His own from moral sickness. So He initiates a conversation with the woman by means of a seemingly simple and obvious request:

> Give me a drink. (John 4:7)

After all, Jesus has just come off a long journey, and presumably it was quite hot, because — as the Gospel tells us — it is "about noon."[1]

The Samaritan woman, in turn, not knowing Who Jesus really is, takes offense at His request. She sees nothing in common with Him; in fact, she sees only differences and hostility! Why speak to Him?

> The Samaritan woman said to Him, "You are a Jew. How can You ask me, a Samaritan and a woman for a drink?" (Recall that Jews have nothing to do with Samaritans.) (John 4:9)

But Jesus had come precisely to be a "peacemaker."[2] So, despite the Samaritan woman's untrusting attitude, He replies with a remark that is obviously meant to stir her curiosity further in regard to Who He really is:

> If only you recognized God's Gift, and Who it is that is asking you for a drink, you would have asked Him instead, and He would have given you Living Water. (John 4:10)

Here Our Lord begins to reveal His hidden identity and all that He could do for her. Because she did not know His true identity and power, she had mistakenly felt she was in a position to control the giving; after all, she could allow Jesus to use her bucket to get Himself a drink of water out of the deep well. In reality, however, it was Jesus Who could give so much more to her than she could ever possibly give to Him. The woman could give water that would quench the thirst of the body; Jesus could give "Living Water," the Holy Spirit, Who could quench the thirst of the soul. The rather stagnant well water would satisfy for a time; the "Living Water" would satisfy for all eternity.

It was obvious that the Samaritan woman did not know Jesus; furthermore, in her sinfulness she could not recognize "the Gift of God," the Holy Spirit! However, once she resolved to turn from her sins, she began to receive the first stirrings of the Holy Spirit. As a result, she excitedly ran off, like a great missionary, and shared the "good news" about Jesus. She enthusiastically told her friends and neighbors all that Jesus had told her. Through her joyful witness, nearly her whole village came to believe in Him.

How many Catholics even today, despite receiving the Holy Spirit both in their Baptism and Confirmation, fully realize or appreciate this priceless treasure? Might not Our Lord's words to the Samaritan woman —"If only you recognized the Gift of God" — also apply to us? What a difference it would make if only we appreciated the Holy Spirit in our daily Christian lives! How much more alive our own faith in Jesus would become. Like the Samaritan woman, we would enthusiastically share the same "good news" about Jesus with those whose lives we touch.

The disciples at Ephesus

A second New Testament example of not appreciating the Holy Spirit involves St. Paul on his third missionary journey. He had just arrived at Ephesus.

> There Paul found some disciples to whom he put the question: "Did you receive the Holy Spirit when you became believers?" They answered, "We have not so much as heard that there is a Holy Spirit." (Acts 19:1-2)

In reality, they had received only the baptism of St. John the Baptist. This was not the Christian Sacrament of Baptism. Rather, it was a sign of accepting the Baptist's message of moral conversion from a life of sin. It also indicated a readiness to accept the promised Messiah Whose mission among the people was about to begin. Apparently this group of disciples had not heard St. John the Baptist say:

> I am baptizing you in water, but there is One to come Who is mightier than I. I am not fit to loosen His sandal strap. He will baptize you in the Holy Spirit and in fire. (Luke 3:16)

St. Paul then taught the group about Jesus and His teaching. Since they believed what he taught them, he baptized them in Jesus' Name. When he then laid hands on them, the Holy Spirit came upon them (Acts 19:4-6).

Perhaps the experience of these disciples reflects a similar situation in the lives of many Catholics today who, through no fault of their own, have received little or no teaching about the Holy Spirit. Maybe it was passed over as unimportant, or as too difficult to present. Or perhaps it was treated so superficially, it left almost no impression at all. As a result, many Catholics today might well echo the surprised statement of those disciples at Ephesus long ago: "We have not so much as heard that there is a Holy Spirit!"

An Example From Church History

Even in Church history, this problem of not appreciating the Holy Spirit's presence and importance in daily Christian life existed! St. Augustine (A.D. 354-430) recognized the lack of theological study regarding the Holy Spirit and His mission even in his own day.

> Many books have been written by scholarly and spiritual men on the Father and the Son... The Holy Spirit has, on the other hand, not yet been studied with as much care and by so many great and learned commentators on the Scriptures that it is easy to understand His special character and know why we cannot call Him either Son or Father, but only Holy Spirit. (*De Fide et Symbolo* IX, #18 & 19: PL 40, 190 and 191)

The theology of the Holy Spirit later became a central focus for St. Augustine. His reflections on the Holy Spirit are found scattered throughout the whole of his later works.

WHY DO WE NOT KNOW THE HOLY SPIRIT AS WE SHOULD?

There are many reasons that account for peoples' failure to appreciate the Holy Spirit. Usually it is a combination of a lack of understanding of Who the Holy Spirit really is and of forgetfulness of His crucial role in our lives as followers of Christ. This is true for many Catholics even today in this post-Vatican Council II period with its renewed interest in the Holy Spirit. For example, a friend told me of an incident that happened when he was at Mass one Pentecost Sunday. When the priest rose to give the homily, he told the congregation in effect: "Since this is Pentecost Sunday you are probably expecting to hear a sermon on the Holy Spirit. But I am not going to give any sermon on the Holy Spirit, because we really don't know that much about Him!" We can only imagine what a discouraging impression his remark must have made on the congregation!

The Notion of Spirit is Mysterious

The first and probably key factor why we do not know the Holy Spirit is that in our human language and experience, we do not relate readily to a "spirit." By contrast, we relate easily to the idea of a "father" and a "son." We know what a human father is, whether through experience (e.g., of our own fathers) and/or observation (e.g., of others as fathers to their own children). We can thus relate to God the Father as a result of our experience and/or observation of human fatherhood.

The same is true with our knowledge of what a human son is. We are all children, sons or daughters, of our own parents. Some of us become parents of our own children. We also observe boys who are sons of other parents. We therefore relate to Jesus as the Son of God from our own human experience and observation.

But we have no experience or observation whatsoever of what a "spirit" is. The very idea of a spirit is the notion of a being without a body, something that has no visible appearance or material makeup. We find this obviously "mysterious." We tend to shy away from what we find awkward to imagine or understand. As a result, many of us feel that we cannot think or talk about the Holy Spirit because we cannot easily relate to Him!

His Mission is Hidden

A second reason for our lack of appreciation of the Holy Spirit is that He is, as Pope John Paul II called Him, the "hidden God." The Second Divine Person, the Son of God, became man by His Incarnation in the womb of the Blessed Virgin Mary. In doing so Jesus took on a visible human appearance by which His disciples knew Him and interacted with Him. They saw Him, heard Him, spoke with Him, touched Him; they were fed by Him, taught by Him, and healed by Him through his physical presence among them.

In contrast, the Holy Spirit took no visible personal form. True, His presence was known at times in various symbolic ways, as by a "dove" at Jesus' baptism in the Jordan (Luke 3:22) and by the "tongues of fire" that accompanied His coming at Pentecost (Acts 2:3). But there was no lasting outward presence. The reason for this was that, although the Spirit was sent to carry on the mission that Jesus had begun among the disciples, He would now do it in a hidden, unseen way. Working in the minds and hearts of those who believed in Jesus, loved Him, and followed Him, the Spirit's presence would remain invisible. Unseen, He carries on the work of forming Christ spiritually in the disciples. This is why Jesus said at the Last Supper:

> I tell you the sober truth: it is much better for you that I go. If I fail to go, the Paraclete will never come to you, whereas if I go, I will send Him to you. When He comes, however, being the Spirit of Truth He will guide you to all truth. (John 16:7, 13)

If Jesus had remained among the disciples in His visible human presence after the Resurrection, their faith would never have grown. After all, faith is the belief in what we do not see. The faith of the Apostles and of Jesus' other first disciples still had to grow, despite His many appearances to them after Easter. Therefore, it was important for Our Lord to withdraw His visible, resurrected presence so that the disciples could continue to grow by believing through faith.[3] This is why Jesus said it was *much better* for the Apostles that He go away from them — precisely so that their faith could grow through the inner working of the Holy Spirit! It would not be easy for the Apostles, after having been with Jesus so long a time, to be deprived of His visible presence. Jesus knew it would cause them sorrow:

> Now that I go back to Him Who sent Me, not one of you asks Me, "Where are You going?" Because I have had all this to say to you, you are overcome with grief. (John 16:5-6)

As is often the case in life, what is best for us is not always easiest for us! But because the Apostles' faith would now grow through a longing desire to see Jesus again and to be reunited with

Him, their love for Him could also grow. This was extremely important because love, as we know, is the virtue that surpasses all the others in dignity; it is the virtue that endures forever!

Despite His going away, however, Jesus would not leave His disciples totally on their own:

> I will not leave you orphaned . . . I will ask the Father and He will give you another Paraclete —to be with you always: the Spirit of Truth . . . (John 14:18, 16-17)

"Paraclete" is a Greek word meaning literally "someone at the side of another person." Jesus had been visibly at the side of His disciples as a constant Teacher and Friend, directing them. He had begun the process of their sanctification — by His preaching and miracles, His personal direction and good example, and by the experiences of His saving death and His post-Resurrection appearances. All of these experiences had been quite visible! Now, the Holy Spirit was to be invisibly at their sides, as a Defender, an Advocate, a Consoler, directing them and fulfilling in them His great mission of making them holy. As a new "Paraclete," the Holy Spirit would direct their continued growth in all the virtues until their holiness was complete. He would strengthen their faith until it became totally unwavering, their hope until it could endure all things, their charity until it became enkindled with great zeal. He would inspire and guide their witnessing of Christ to the very ends of the earth, even in the face of rejection, persecution, suffering, and death itself. The Holy Spirit would do all of this in a manner that was quiet, unseen, hidden, but nevertheless, very real and quite effective. His presence would be known, not by any outward human form, but by observing the effects of His hidden presence working in and through them.

THE IMPORTANCE OF KNOWING "THE GIFT OF GOD"

Because we cannot see the Holy Spirit, we can easily forget what an important role He plays in our lives as followers of Jesus.

Therefore, in spite of the difficulties in getting to know the Holy Spirit, it is very important that we do so. After all, it is precisely through the presence and work of the Holy Spirit in us that we live our Christian life.

> If anyone does not have the Spirit of Christ, he does not belong to Christ . . . All who are led by the Spirit of God are sons of God. (Romans 8:9, 14)

THE APOSTLES' NEED FOR THE HOLY SPIRIT

This point becomes even clearer as we look closely at the need the Apostles themselves had for the Holy Spirit. Jesus was sending the Paraclete, first of all, to continue their personal growth in holiness. No doubt, the Apostles received abundant graces in knowing Jesus in close, personal friendship on earth. They had been with Our Lord during the three years of His public ministry. They were privileged to see the Risen Lord on many occasions after He rose from the dead on Easter. Yet, they still needed the grace of the Holy Spirit to complete the work of sanctification Jesus had begun in them. Our Lord very clearly presented this need as He was ready to ascend into Heaven to His place of glory at the right hand of His Heavenly Father. He gave the Apostles this final instruction:

> Wait for the fulfillment of My Father's promise of which you have heard Me speak. John baptized with water, but within a few days you will be baptized with the Holy Spirit . . . You will receive power when the Holy Spirit comes down on you; then you are to be My witnesses in Jerusalem, throughout Judea and Samaria, yes, even to the ends of the earth. (Acts 1:4-5, 8)

In addition to their own personal growth in holiness, Our Lord gave them a tremendous apostolic work. He commissioned them to be His "witnesses" even to the very ends of the earth. This was an enormous undertaking. It was a worldwide preaching mission. In order to accomplish it, they needed the power and strength of the

Spirit. Our Lord Himself refers to the Holy Spirit as "power from on high" (Luke 24:49). Furthermore, they would need the Spirit's constant guidance and encouragement and the support of His gifts.

No wonder Our Lord did not want the Apostles to leave Jerusalem until they had received the "Gift" and "Promise" of the Father. They could only leave when the promised Holy Spirit had been poured forth upon them. Our Lord instructed them in this way because He knew all the difficulties that awaited them as they preached the Gospel message, calling people to conversion and eternal life.

The Example of St. Paul as an Apostle

Let us look at the experience of St. Paul. It clearly illustrates the difficulties that the Apostles in general endured for the sake of the Gospel.

To brave the dangers of travel

First, there were his dangers in traveling. He enumerated many of the sufferings he endured in his travels: three times he was shipwrecked; one time he passed a whole day and a whole night adrift on the sea; he was always in danger from wild animals, floods, and other hazards as he went from city to city preaching the Gospel (2 Corinthians 11:25-26). Such inconveniences and hardships were part of the life and experience of any true apostle of the Lord: hunger and thirst, cold and heat, sleepless nights and homelessness, from town to town.

To face opposition

Then there was constant opposition and even persecution. St. Paul, for example, had little groups of opponents following him from town to town, and heckling him as he tried to speak to the people. Sometimes they maliciously stirred up the crowds and turned them against him. At other times St. Paul experienced humiliation, such as the time he spoke to the people at Athens (Acts 17:16-34). They literally laughed him out of town for preaching about the resurrection of the body. He left the city of Athens deeply frustrated!

To handle discouragement

Added to all these difficulties were situations of sadness and discouragement that St. Paul experienced. These occurred, for example, when some of his disciples, who at one time believed, later turned away in disbelief. His Letter to the Galatians clearly reflects the great sorrow and distress he felt as he saw the community of disciples there abandoning the Faith he had taught them and accepting instead what he called "another gospel" (= heretical teachings; cf. Galatians 1:6).

To endure physical sufferings

Finally, St. Paul experienced many physical sufferings for Jesus' sake. He spoke about his own imprisonment, his receiving thirty-nine lashes on five occasions, his three times being beaten with rods, and his once even being stoned and left for dead! (2 Corinthians 11:23-5).

OUR OWN NEED FOR THE HOLY SPIRIT

To face all these sufferings — and they were great — Our Lord knew that all of His Apostles would require the constant strength and renewal coming to them through the grace of the Holy Spirit.

We, too, need this same grace of the Holy Spirit. We may not have to face the same trials as the Apostles, but we have our own. These we must likewise endure for the love of Christ and His Church. We must be strengthened and refreshed by the Holy Spirit's consolation, guided by His enlightenment, and fortified by His courage. It is no wonder that the Scriptures refer to the Holy Spirit as "the Gift of God," Whom we must come to know in our own daily lives.

Footnotes

1. Although it was only natural for Him to experience a burning thirst, the request of Our Lord really had a much deeper meaning. It actually arose not from any physical thirst on His part, but from a spiritual thirst. It was an expression of His burning desire for this woman's salvation! It was similar to His cry on the cross:

   I thirst. (John 19:28)

   Indeed, many early Christian writers known as the Fathers of the Church, saw this plea as Jesus' "thirsting" or yearning for the salvation of all men and women for whom He was at that very moment giving His life on the Cross. He had said that this was precisely why He would be lifted up on a cross in crucifixion:

   And I — once I am lifted up from the earth —will draw all men to Myself. (John 12:32)

2. In fact, St. Paul later described Jesus as "our Peace," the One Who unites all of us despite our differences. He writes of how Jesus had broken down the differences that had previously separated many of His disciples, like Jews from Gentiles, and how He had become the bridge or link now uniting them in a common bond of faith and life in Himself:

   He is our Peace, Who would make the two of us one by breaking down the barrier of hostility that kept us apart. (Ephesians 2:14)

3. This was an important part of Jesus' testing the faith of St. Thomas the Apostle, who at first doubted His Resurrection. On that occasion Jesus blessed all those who did not see but still believed!

Chapter 2

Obtaining the Holy Spirit:
Gift and Gift-Giver

THE HOLY SPIRIT DIRECTS US toward the fullness of redemption promised us by Jesus by sharing with us His gifts. In a sense, the Holy Spirit Himself is the Supreme Gift; but He is also the Giver of other gifts. The gifts of the Holy Spirit are often divided into two kinds: the "sevenfold gifts" and the "charismatic gifts."

HIS SEVENFOLD GIFTS FOR OUR SANCTIFICATION

The first kind of gifts of the Holy Spirit are the sevenfold gifts mentioned by the prophet Isaiah:

> But a shoot shall sprout from the stump of Jesse and from his roots a bud shall blossom. The spirit of the Lord shall rest upon Him: a spirit of wisdom and of understanding, a spirit of counsel and of strength, a spirit of knowledge and of fear of the Lord, and His delight shall be the fear of the Lord. (Isaiah 11:1-3)[1]

These gifts come to us along with the Holy Spirit Himself at the time of our Baptism. These seven gifts are used by the Holy Spirit to help a person grow in holiness. They are directed at our personal sanctification. They make us more sensitive to receive and carry out the inspirations and promptings of the Holy Spirit. Four of them, Wisdom, Knowledge, Understanding, and Counsel, assist

15

our minds to know God and the truths of our Catholic Faith more clearly. The other three gifts, Courage, Piety, and Fear of the Lord, assist our will and strengthen us to love God more ardently.

HIS CHARISMATIC GIFTS TO BUILD UP THE MYSTICAL BODY

The second category of gifts of the Holy Spirit are the so-called "charismatic gifts." These gifts are not for our personal growth in holiness. Rather, they are given to individual persons to help build up the Church, the "Mystical Body of Christ." St. Paul listed some of these charismatic gifts when he wrote to the Christian community at Corinth:

> To each person the manifestation of the Spirit is given for the common good. To one the Spirit gives wisdom in discourse, to another the power to express knowledge. Through the Spirit one receives faith; by the same Spirit another is given the gift of healing, and still another miraculous powers. Prophecy is given to one; to another power to distinguish one spirit from another. One receives the gift of tongues, another that of interpreting the tongues. But it is one and the same Spirit Who produces all these gifts, distributing them to each as He wills.
> (1 Corinthians 12:7-11)

St. Paul's teaching here is that, because different individuals possess different charismatic gifts, the community as a whole possesses a fullness of the Spirit's charismatic gifts. Therefore, whatever need may arise in the community at large, one or another individual will probably possess a special gift to help meet that need. Let us look at a few examples of these charismatic gifts.

A person with the gift of "wisdom in discourse" has an exceptional ability to teach the truths of the Faith with clarity and facility to well-educated Catholics as well as to those who have never received proper religious instruction. A person with the gift to "distinguish one spirit from another" is able to discern whether something is actually coming from the Holy Spirit, from the Evil

Spirit, or from an individual's own human spirit. In other words, someone with this gift is usually able to distinguish whether something is coming genuinely from God, from a deceit of the Devil, or from a conscious or unconscious level within an individual person. Another charismatic gift is that of "miraculous powers."[2] Someone with this gift is able to edify both believers and non-believers alike with miraculous signs and wonders, strengthening the faith of those who already believe and leading to faith those who do not yet believe.

In summary, we need to have the sevenfold or sanctifying gifts of the Holy Spirit for our own personal growth in holiness. We also need those charismatic gifts which the Holy Spirit may choose to give us so that we may share in the work of the Church and help to realize God's plan of salvation for the world. When all the members of the Church with their particular gifts work together, the unity of the Church is more deeply expressed, and her work bears more abundant fruit.

THE HOLY SPIRIT AT OUR BAPTISM AND CONFIRMATION

We received the Holy Spirit, the Gift of God, for the first time in the new supernatural life conferred on us through our Baptism. We received Him again in a special way when our Christian lives reached a certain maturity at Confirmation. We may ask if we can continue to receive a fuller measure of the Spirit and His working in our daily lives. The answer emphatically is "Yes"!

We must realize that when we speak of receiving a "fuller measure" of the Holy Spirit, we do not mean this in terms of an increase of "quantity," like something increasing in ounces or feet. Since the Holy Spirit is a Divine Person, He is completely present in us all at once. There is no "increase" of presence on His part. The "increase," if we may call it that, is on our part. It simply means we become more aware of His presence, more open to use His graces and more docile to follow out His inspirations.

The "Down-payment" of Our Redemption

It is interesting that St. Paul in his writings refers to the Holy Spirit once as the "first fruits" (Romans 8:23) of our redemption and twice as the "first payment" (what we call today "the down payment") of our redemption (2 Corinthians 1:22; Ephesians 1:14). As an example, he writes to the Church at Ephesus:

> In Him (Christ) you too were chosen; when you heard the glad tidings of salvation, the word of truth, and believed in it, you were sealed with the Holy Spirit Who had been promised. He is the pledge of our inheritance, the first payment against the full redemption of the people God has made His own to praise His glory. (Ephesians 1:13-14)

What St. Paul means by these expressions is that the presence of the Holy Spirit within us marks the beginning of our redemption. A "down payment" is the first installment given in the purchase of something; other payments will follow. The Holy Spirit is this "first payment of our redemption" because through His working in us, more of His gifts will be bestowed upon us. We will finally come to the full sharing in the redemption that Christ has won for us when we enter the Kingdom of Heaven.[3]

The "first fruits" marks only the beginning of the harvest; the fullness of the harvest will follow. In a similar way, the bestowing of the Holy Spirit upon us marks only the beginning of the effects of Christ's Redemption. Again, we will experience the fullness of the harvest of Redemption in Heaven. Furthermore, the "first fruits" is usually among the choicest portions of the harvest. Along with many other gifts to us, preeminently the Holy Eucharist, the Sacraments, Sanctifying Grace, the Church, and Our Lady, the Holy Spirit is God's most precious Gift to us.

THE NEED TO PRAY FOR "THE GIFT OF GOD"

The chief means to obtain this "Gift of God" is through constant prayer. It is interesting to compare an aspect of Jesus' teaching on prayer as recorded both in St. Matthew and in St. Luke. Both Gospel accounts express Jesus' teaching that in prayer we are to ask, to seek, and to knock at the door. But now let us compare what follows:

> If you, with all your sins know how to give your children what is good, how much more will your heavenly Father give good things to anyone who asks Him! (Matthew 7:11)

> If you, with all your sins, know how to give your children good things, how much more will the heavenly Father give the Holy Spirit to those who ask Him. (Luke 11:13)

Note what gifts the Father gives in each Gospel teaching. St. Matthew tells us that the Heavenly Father gives "good things" to those who ask Him. These "good things" obviously include both our physical goods, such as food, clothing, shelter, and good weather, as well as our spiritual goods, such as His love, patience, mercy, and grace to overcome our sins and temptations. St. Luke tells us that the Heavenly Father gives us simply the "Holy Spirit." Why? Because the Holy Spirit is the chief Gift that God gives to His people; in fact, along with the Holy Spirit, the Heavenly Father gives us all other good things. We can easily conclude from St. Luke's account that Our Lord encourages us to pray to the Heavenly Father for the Gift of the Holy Spirit.

As good proof of this we can ask: What did the Apostles do as they waited in Jerusalem after Ascension Thursday for the promised Gift of the Holy Spirit? According to the Acts of the Apostles, they gathered to pray:

> After that they returned to Jerusalem from the Mount called Olivet near Jerusalem — a mere Sabbath's journey away. Entering the city, they went to the upstairs room where they were staying. Peter and John and James and Andrew; Philip

and Thomas, Bartholomew and Matthew; James, son of Alphaeus, Simon, the Zealot party member, and Judas, son of James. Together they devoted themselves to constant prayer. There were some women in their company, and Mary, the Mother of Jesus, and His brothers. (Acts 1:12-14)

The Apostles joined Our Lady and the other first disciples (about one hundred twenty persons in all) and they prayed together for the grace of the Holy Spirit.[4] The nine days intervening between Ascension Thursday and Pentecost Sunday became the Church's first novena. It was a novena to receive the grace of the Holy Spirit as Jesus had promised.

St. Francis, a very faithful follower of Our Lord, also stressed the importance of prayer for the Gift of the Holy Spirit. He put into his Rule for the friars an important exhortation on this point.

Let the friars endeavor to have what is to be above all things desired, the Spirit of the Lord and His holy operation; let them endeavor to pray always with a pure heart. (Rule of 1223, Ch. 10)

St. Francis' words should inspire us to pray daily for the grace of the Holy Spirit. His teaching and his own example would certainly encourage all of us to pray with enthusiastic longing and heartfelt desire for this most wonderful Gift of God to us.

We find in the Church's "Liturgy of the Hours" an inspiring hymn that expresses this desire for the Gift of God:[5]

Father, Lord of earth and heaven,
King to Whom all gifts belong,
Give Your greatest Gift, Your Spirit,
God the holy, God the strong.

Son of God, enthroned in Glory,
Send Your promised Gift of Grace,
Make Your Church, Your Holy Temple,
God the Spirit's dwelling-place.

Spirit, come, in peace descending,
As at Jordan heavenly Dove,

Seal Your Church as God's anointed,
Set our hearts on fire with love.

Stay among us, God the Father,
Stay among us, God the Son,
Stay among us, Holy Spirit,
Dwell within us, make us one.

(Melody by Drakes Boughton; Music by E. Elgar, 1857-1934; Text by James
Quinn, S.J., copyright James Quinn, S.J., from *New Hymns For All Seasons*,
published by Geoffrey Chapman, London and quoted in *Christian Prayer:
The Liturgy of the Hours*, copyright 1976 by the Daughters of St. Paul and
used with permission.)

THE GIFT OF THE SPIRIT IS GIVEN ABUNDANTLY

The Lord is always ready to give the Gift of the Holy Spirit to us, and He is willing to give it in abundance.

For the One Whom God has sent speaks the words of God; He does not ration His Gift of the Spirit. (John 3:34)

This verse tells us that Jesus is the One Whom the Father has sent and Who speaks the Father's words or message to us. It is also Jesus Who does not ration His Gift of the Spirit, but rather pours that Gift into our hearts in superabundance. God is never miserly in giving His gifts. However, sometimes we might be quite limited in our capacity to receive them. But it is always God's desire to be very generous with what He shares with us.

This point is made in an interesting story found in the Old Testament Book of Numbers. It involves a situation in which Moses, who has been leading the Jewish people through the desert, has become discouraged. He has been burdened by the constant complaints of the Israelites in the desert, one complaint after another. So he comes to God in prayer and asks:

Why are You so displeased with me that You burden me with all this people? Was it I who conceived all this people? Or was it I who gave them birth, that You tell me to carry them at my bosom, like a foster father carrying an infant, to the land You have promised under oath to their fathers? (Numbers 11:11-12)

The Lord hears Moses' prayer and responds:

Assemble for Me seventy of the elders of Israel.... I will take some of this spirit that is on you and will bestow it on them, that they may share the burden of the people with you. You will then not have to bear it by yourself. (Numbers 11: 16-17)

Conveying God's message to the people, Moses selects the seventy men who will assist him in governing the people. He gathers them around the meeting tent. God then appears in a cloud and speaks to Moses. He shares the spirit of leadership that He had poured upon Moses with these seventy other helpers:

Taking some of the spirit that was on Moses, He bestowed it on the seventy elders; and as the spirit came to rest on them, they prophesied. (Numbers 11:25)[6]

After the seventy elders receive the Spirit that had been on Moses alone, the following incident occurs:

Now two men, one named Eldad and the other Medad, were not in the gathering but had been left in the camp. They too had been on the list but had not gone out to the tent; yet the spirit came to rest on them also, and they prophesied in the camp. So when a young man quickly told Moses, "Eldad and Medad are prophesying in the camp," Joshua, son of Nun, who from his youth had been Moses' aide, said, "Moses, my lord, stop them." But Moses answered him, "Are you jealous for my sake? Would that all the people of the Lord were prophets! Would that the Lord might bestow His spirit on them all!" (Numbers 11:26-30)

We see in this last episode a contrast between the young man Joshua and the old man Moses. Joshua was jealous of the authority of Moses over all the people. When he heard that Eldad and Medad had received a share in the spirit of Moses and that they were prophesying, he wanted Moses to command them to stop. In this way, Moses would have shown that he had authority over them, even though they were not with him when they received a share in his spirit. Perhaps Joshua's outlook could be attributed to his youth, inexperience, and impulsiveness. In his youthfulness, he lacked a certain broadening of outlook that comes with maturing in the spiritual life. His vision was too narrow, his feelings too jealous and insecure. Without realizing it, he was putting limits on the Spirit of God. He was "rationing" the Gift of God.

Moses, by contrast, is a symbol of one who had matured greatly in the spiritual life. Through his intense union with God by way of fervent prayer and through the many trials he endured during the Exodus, leading the people to the Promised Land, he had certainly grown in great charity, both for God and his neighbor. So when young Joshua told him to command Eldad and Medad to cease prophesying, Moses took just the opposite point of view. There was no narrow-heartedness caused by jealousy for his own prestige, nor any insecurity that his authority was being challenged, nor was there any sadness from envy of what others had come to possess. Rather, with true magnanimity in his heart, he rejoiced that others, too, could share in a generous portion of the divine Gift of the Spirit. He only wished that God had poured forth His Spirit on all the people!

Certainly this same Gift of the Holy Spirit is waiting for all of us, too, just for the asking! And this Gift will not be rationed to us, but poured forth abundantly into our hearts.

Footnotes

1. The prophet Isaiah foretold that the "Servant" Who was expected to come (a reference to Jesus as the offshoot of Jesse) would possess the seven gifts of the Spirit of the Lord. Note that the gift of the "Fear of the Lord" is mentioned here twice; however, we generally understand the first reference as the Spirit's gift of Piety, and the second reference as His gift of the Fear of the Lord.
2. A miracle is an occurrence in which an effect is produced that goes completely beyond the natural powers of the person involved (e.g., an instantaneous healing of a terminal disease, the sudden changing of one substance into another, such as water into wine), and it defies any natural explanation.
3. The Church in her Liturgy expresses this thought in Eucharistic Prayer IV. This prayer gives a very brief outline of the ministry of Christ leading up to His death and to His

pouring forth of the Gift of the Holy Spirit. We pray in this Eucharistic Prayer:

In fulfillment of Your will He (Jesus) gave Himself up to death; but by rising from the dead, He destroyed death and restored life. And that we might live no longer for ourselves but for Him, He sent the Holy Spirit from You, Father, as His first Gift to those who believe, to complete His work on earth and bring us the fullness of grace.

4. It is important to note that Mary was there. We, too, should try daily to ask Our Blessed Lady to intercede that we might receive a greater share of the Gift of the Holy Spirit.
5. It is found among the hymns recommended for what is called "Mid-Morning Prayer," a prayer hour which corresponds to 9 a.m. Interestingly, this particular hour of prayer is dedicated to the Holy Spirit because the Holy Spirit descended on Pentecost at about 9 a.m. (Acts 2:15).
6. With the help of the Holy Spirit and His gifts, like that of prophecy, these seventy elders assisted Moses in caring for God's people. Interestingly, the Church refers to this same story in the prayer of ordination of new priests. These new priests receive the Gift of the Holy Spirit through their priestly Ordination, enabling them to assist their bishop in teaching, governing, and sanctifying the members of the Church committed to their spiritual care.

Chapter 3

Fervent Devotion to the Holy Spirit

IN ORDER TO GET A COMPLETE PICTURE of devotion to the Holy Spirit, we must look at the whole of the Church's history. It is encouraging to find that there have been many periods of great awareness of the Holy Spirit and His guidance of the Church. There have also been countless individuals who have had a deep personal devotion to the Third Person of the Blessed Trinity. On the other hand, there have been both movements and individuals who rejected the Holy Spirit or distorted devotion to Him. In this chapter, we will look at some of these aspects of fervor in regard to devotion to the Holy Spirit throughout the Church's history, while in the following chapter we will examine certain elements of decline.

THE APOSTOLIC CHURCH

Pentecost is the supreme example of both awareness and devotion to the Holy Spirit in the Church. This was the day when that first group of disciples, approximately 120 in all, including Our Lady, the Apostles, and various relatives of the Lord (Acts 1:13-15), were united to form the nucleus of God's new people by the great outpouring of the Holy Spirit upon them. Later that day, after St. Peter and the other Apostles had finished preaching to the vast crowd that had gathered at the Holy Spirit's descent, three thousand more people came to believe, and they were baptized! Pentecost was truly "the birthday of the Church."

The Acts of the Apostles bears witness to the great consciousness the first generation of Christians had of the presence and working of the Holy Spirit in their midst. It has sometimes been called "The Gospel of the Holy Spirit."

Ample evidence of the Holy Spirit and the working of His gifts is reflected in the letters written by St. Paul to the various Church communities he established. One of the most outstanding of these is his First Letter to the Corinthians which focuses a great deal of attention on the Holy Spirit and His charismatic gifts. Romans 8 stresses the Spirit's role in our prayer life, enabling us to address God as "Abba" (Father), and Galatians 5 emphasizes the fruits of the Spirit as opposed to those of the flesh. These are significant for our understanding of the vital presence of the Holy Spirit in our lives as Christians.

THROUGHOUT THE CENTURIES

Throughout the Church's history, the role of the Holy Spirit has been highlighted. St. Cyril, bishop of Jerusalem (A.D. 315-386), wrote in beautiful imagery about the many varied effects or fruits of the Holy Spirit in the lives of each one of us. He compared the Holy Spirit to rain, which is the same wherever it comes down. However, the rain produces different fruits and flowers according to the kinds of plants it waters. So, too, in the Church community, it is the same Holy Spirit Who comes to each person. But He brings forth different effects in each person's life, according to their different circumstances, needs, and gifts. In one of his famous catechetical instructions, St. Cyril of Jerusalem wrote:

> "The water that I shall give him will become in him a fountain of living water, welling up into eternal life" (John 4:14). This is a new kind of water, a living, leaping water, welling up for those who are worthy. But why did Christ call the grace of the

Spirit water? Because all things are dependent on water; plants and animals have their origin in water. Water comes down from heaven as rain, and although it is always the same in itself, it produces many different effects, one in the palm tree, another in the vine, and so on throughout the whole of creation. It does not come down, now as one thing, now as another, but while remaining essentially the same, it adapts itself to the needs of every creature that receives it.

In the same way, the Holy Spirit whose nature is always the same, simple and indivisible, apportions grace to each man as He wills. Like a dry tree which puts forth shoots when watered, the soul bears the fruit of holiness when repentance has made it worthy of receiving the Holy Spirit. Although the Spirit never changes, the effects of His action, by the will of God and in the name of Christ, are both many and marvelous. The Spirit makes one man a teacher of divine truth, inspires another to prophesy, gives another the power of casting out devils, enables another to interpret holy Scripture. The Spirit strengthens one man's self-control, shows another how to help the poor, teaches another to fast and lead a life of asceticism, makes another oblivious to the needs of the body, trains another for martyrdom. His action is different in different people, but the Spirit Himself is always the same. "In each person," Scripture says, "the Spirit reveals His presence in a particular way for the common good" (1 Corinthians 12:7). (From a catechetical instruction by Saint Cyril of Jerusalem, bishop, Cat. 16, *De Spiritu Sancto* 1, 11-12, 16: PG 33, 931-935, 939-942)

The Early Martyrs

The martyrs of the first centuries often faced cruel suffering and death conscious of the strength the Holy Spirit would give them. The list of the martyrs of the early Church seems almost endless. Great names appear among them. There were men such as St. Clement of Rome, St. Ignatius of Antioch, St. Polycarp, St. Irenaeus, and St. Cyprian. There were also many women who suffered martyrdom with great courage, such as St. Felicity, St. Perpetua, St. Agatha, St. Agnes, and St. Lucy.

A good example of the heroism of the early martyrs is found in the account of the trial of St. Justin the Martyr and several companions. When a Roman prefect, Rusticus, had commanded them to offer sacrifice to the pagan gods, they steadfastly refused. Rusticus then interrogated St. Justin as spokesman for the group:

> Rusticus said: "What system of teaching do you profess?" Justin said, "I have tried to learn about every system, but I have accepted the true doctrines of the Christians, though these are not approved by those who are held fast by error . . ."
> Rusticus said: "You are a Christian, then?" Justin said, "Yes, I am a Christian . . ."
> The prefect Rusticus said, "Do you have an idea that (if you were scourged and beheaded) you will go up to heaven to receive some suitable reward?" Justin said: "It is not an idea that I have; it is something I know well and hold to be most certain . . ."
> The prefect Rusticus said: "Now let us come to the point at issue . . . offer sacrifice to the gods . . . If you do not do as you are commanded you will be tortured without mercy." Justin said: "We hope to suffer torment for the sake of our Lord Jesus Christ and so be saved. For this will bring us salvation and confidence as we stand before the more terrible and universal judgment seat of our Lord and Savior."
> In the same way the other martyrs also said: "Do what you will. We are Christians; we do not offer sacrifice to idols."
> (From the *Acts of the Martyrdom of St. Justin and his Companion Saints*, Cap. 1-5; cf. PG 6, 1366-1371)

St. Justin and his companions were then sentenced to be scourged, and they died as martyrs by being beheaded! The courage to remain steadfast in the face of such threats and ultimately to experience the sufferings of martyrdom certainly had to have been the effects of the Holy Spirit within them.

The Fathers of the Church

In addition to the martyrs, there was also a courageous group known as the Fathers of the Church. For approximately the first seven centuries of Christianity, they sought the Spirit's wisdom and knowledge to combat various heresies that had arisen within the Church communities as well as to establish peace and order where there had been internal strife. They were generally known for their great learning and sanctity in the early Church, and include some of the greatest spiritual giants of the Catholic Faith. Among their number were St. Jerome, St. Ambrose, St. Basil the Great, St. John Chrysostom, St. Athanasius, St. Gregory the Great, and probably the greatest of them all, St. Augustine. Their writings often reflect such depth of understanding, such useful guidance for Christian living, and such spiritual beauty and delight that they definitely could not have been written without the enlightenment and assistance of the Holy Spirit.

One example, perhaps less known than many of the others, is St. Ephraem the Deacon (c. 306-c. 379). Born in ancient Mesopotamia (modern Iraq), he lived for a while also in Syria, and he died at Edessa. He possessed gifts of natural eloquence and poetry. He was an outstanding defender of the Catholic Faith, courageously opposing various heresies. Many of his writings were in the form of hymns for the liturgy and poems to instruct the people in the Catholic Faith. This won for him the popular nickname, "the harp of the Holy Spirit." St. Jerome once read a work by St. Ephraem on the Holy Spirit and declared:

> St. Ephraem, deacon of the Church of Edessa, wrote many works in Syriac, and became so famous that his writings are publicly read in some churches after the Sacred Scriptures. I have read in Greek a volume of his on the Holy Spirit; though it was only a translation, I recognized therein the sublime genius of the man. (*De Viris Illustribus*, c. 115)

Founders of Various Religious Communities

The Holy Spirit was also at work inspiring different forms of religious life. In the beginning, there was the emergence of monasticism, from its humble origins in the deserts of Egypt and Palestine to the great monastic tradition of the Basilian and Benedictine monks that has lasted over 1500 years. Later, in what has been called the "Golden Age" of the Middle Ages, the 13th Century, there came the emergence of new forms of religious life with the mendicant friars, such as the Dominican, Carmelite and Franciscan Orders. Still later came other forms of religious life, such as the Jesuits, the Redemptorists and the Salesians. Even in our day, we have witnessed the worldwide emergence of the Missionaries of Charity.

Such founders as St. Basil, St. Benedict, St. Francis, St. Dominic, St. Simon Stock, St. Ignatius Loyola, St. Alphonsus Liguori, and St. John Bosco, among the men, and St. Scholastica, St. Clare, St. Teresa of Avila, St. Jane Frances de Chantal, and Mother Teresa of Calcutta, among the women, have truly been persons open to the guidance and inspiration of the Holy Spirit as they worked either to establish or to reform their respective communities. As an example of these religious founders, we shall later focus on the Holy Spirit in the life of St. Francis of Assisi.

Great Mystics and Spiritual Writers

The Holy Spirit also guided the writings of great mystics and spiritual authors, such as St. Bernard, St. Bonaventure, St. Thomas Aquinas, St. Catherine of Siena, St. Teresa of Avila, St. John of the Cross, St. Francis de Sales, and St. Therese of Lisieux. Their writings possess a remarkable insight into the spiritual life. Furthermore, they seem to be able to write with ease and clarity about some of the deepest and most obscure mystical realities. No doubt they could do this only because they had already personally experienced them by the working of the Holy Spirit. Their clarity, conviction, and attractiveness have moved many to pursue a life of holiness.

One clear example of the influence of the Holy Spirit on these mystical writers occurred in the life of St. Teresa of Avila. It happened while she was writing her masterpiece, *The Interior Castle*, a book about progress in prayer and growth through various stages of holiness. In her book she shared her need to pray to the Holy Spirit for enlightenment as she prepared to explain the deep concept of mystical prayer:

> In order to begin to speak of the fourth dwelling places I really need to entrust myself, as I've already done, to the Holy Spirit and beg Him to speak for me from here on that I may say something about the remaining rooms in a way that you will understand. For supernatural experiences begin here. These are something most difficult to explain, if His Majesty doesn't do so . . . Although I think I now have a little more light about these favors the Lord grants to some souls, knowing how to explain them is a different matter. May His Majesty help me to do so if it will be of some benefit . . . (*Teresa of Avila: The Interior Castle*, IV Chap. 1, p. 67; Classics of Western Spirituality, Paulist Press, NY: 1979)

In another place, she restated her need for the help of the Holy Spirit to write:

> May He be pleased that I manage to explain something about these very difficult things. I know well that this will be impossible if His Majesty and the Holy Spirit do not move my pen. (*Ibid.*, V, Chap. 4, no. 11, pp. 106-107)

Finally, we have the witness of some of those who knew St. Teresa as she was writing the *Interior Castle*. There is testimony that she seemed to be inspired, no doubt by the Holy Spirit, as she did her actual writing of the book. Here is the testimony of a woman named Maria del Nacimiento:

> When the said Mother Teresa of Jesus wrote the book called *The Dwelling Places* (*Interior Castle*) she was in Toledo, and this witness saw that it was after Communion that she wrote this book, and when she wrote, she did so very rapidly and with such great beauty in her countenance that this witness was in

admiration, and she was so absorbed in what she was writing that even if some noise was made there, it did not hinder her; wherefore this witness understood that in all that which she wrote and during the time she was writing, she was in prayer. (see Silverio de Santo Teresa, *Biblioteca Mistica Carmelitana*, vol. 18 [Burgos: El Monte Carmelo, 1934], p. 315 as quoted in *Ibid.*, Introduction, p. 19)

In Times of Reform and Renewal in the Church

The Holy Spirit was also at work in times of reform and renewal. An outstanding example of this is the Catholic Reformation at the time of the Council of Trent. It was a time when the whole Church needed renewal. Guided by the Holy Spirit, the bishops at Trent enacted much needed legislation calling for reform, especially through the elimination of abuses. They passed laws to guide the bishops in the running of their dioceses, thereby eliminating the widespread abuse of absentee bishops. They called for the establishment of seminaries for the proper education and formation of future priests. This was so necessary because ignorance and laxity on the part of many clergy had been the source of much neglect and even scandal. The Council also issued legislation for the reform of similar abuses in religious communities. While condemning different heresies that had been proposed by the Protestant leaders, the Council provided for the proper instruction of the laity by issuing a catechism on the teachings of the Catholic Church.

In this same period of time, the Holy Spirit inspired the emergence of new Religious Orders. The most outstanding were the Jesuits whose work in education and the missions proved to be a great source of renewal in the Church. The Holy Spirit also guided the reforms of various existing communities. Among the Franciscans, the Capuchin reform began, and it was to have an enormous effect on Church renewal through the popular preaching of the friars. St. Teresa of Avila and St. John of the Cross initiated the reform of the Carmelite nuns and friars. The Holy Spirit had truly breathed new life and fervor into the Church.

VATICAN COUNCIL II

In our own day we have become very aware of a new outpouring of the Holy Spirit upon the Church through the Second Vatican Council. When Pope John XXIII convoked the Vatican Council, he certainly startled the world. Perhaps this was in keeping with his own personality since he himself was a kind of delightful surprise. He did things people did not expect. For example, he was known to leave the confines of Vatican City, donning the simple black cassock and round hat that were characteristic of the priests of Rome. He would walk unrecognized through the streets in Rome. It was said that many times even the Swiss guards at the Vatican did not know the whereabouts of the Pope. A delightful story is told of how Pope John once stopped at a Catholic hospital called the "Hospital of the Holy Spirit" located not too far from the Vatican. The Mother Superior of the hospital, its administrator, was also the anesthetist for the hospital. She was on duty during an operation when she was informed that the Holy Father had made a surprise visit to the hospital. Unable to leave the operating room, she gave word to the person next in charge to take the Holy Father around and show him every courtesy. She indicated she would join them as soon as she could. When the operation was over, the Mother Superior dashed out of the operating room, came into the presence of the Holy Father, and greeted him quite excitedly, "Your Holiness, I am the Mother Superior of the Holy Spirit!" The Pope looked at her and said, "Mother, you are doing better than I am; I am only the Vicar of Christ!"

It is significant to remember that Pope John XXIII was a Church historian. He had even taught Church History for a while in the seminary. He realized that the life of the Church and the life of the people in our society were moving further and further apart. He was afraid that the Church was losing her ability to speak meaningfully to the world of today. He stated that his purpose in invoking a new Ecumenical Council was to "update" the Church. He wanted to stir up the revitalizing power of the Holy Spirit.[1]

Pope John also prayed that the Second Vatican Council would become a "Second Pentecost" in the Church. His prayer was answered; the Second Vatican Council has providentially led to a greater awareness of the Holy Spirit in the Church today. There have been many expressions of this. Perhaps the most outstanding example has been the "Catholic Charismatic Movement" through which people have become more aware of the Holy Spirit and His gifts working in their lives. This has generally been a very positive force also for the renewal of prayer in the Church today.

We do not, however, have to be members of the Charismatic Renewal or even of a prayer group to experience the Holy Spirit's power at work in our lives. Through the Sacraments of Baptism and Confirmation we have already received the outpouring of the Holy Spirit into our hearts. Through His inspiration and grace, we can all bear the fruits that are the signs of His presence and power in our Christian lives.

> The fruit of the Spirit is love, joy, peace, patient endurance, kindness, generosity, faith, mildness and chastity. (Galatians 5:22-23)

DEVOTION OF INDIVIDUALS TO THE HOLY SPIRIT

Besides these periods and events in the Church's history that express a deep awareness of the Holy Spirit's presence and power, there have also been individuals whose lives have been marked by great devotion and openness to the Holy Spirit. Although there are countless examples of this among the lives of our saints, the life of St. Francis of Assisi expresses a special openness to the presence and working of the Holy Spirit within him.

The Example of St. Francis

St. Francis' biography was written by one of his outstanding followers, St. Bonaventure.[2] He shares many instances of St. Francis' experiences of the Holy Spirit.

The first reference occurs at the very beginning of St. Francis' conversion, while he was still caught up with the things of the world. St. Bonaventure tells us that adversity is one of the chief tools God uses to sharpen the spiritual awareness of people. Accordingly, God permitted suffering to afflict St. Francis in order to prepare him to receive a generous outpouring of the Holy Spirit.

> The fire of divine love was never extinguished in Francis' heart, but as a young man he was taken up with the cares of this world and could not grasp the hidden message contained in God's words. Then the hand of God came upon him; he suffered a prolonged and distressing illness, while his heart was enlightened by the infusion of the Holy Spirit. (*The Minor Life*, Chapter 1, Lesson 2)

St. Francis had a second experience of the Holy Spirit while praying before an image of Christ crucified, in a little chapel called "San Damiano" (St. Damian's). Our Lord spoke to Francis from the cross, giving him the mission to rebuild His Church.

> St. Francis left the town of Assisi one day to meditate out of doors and, as he was passing by the church of San Damiano, which was threatening to collapse with age, he was inspired by the Holy Spirit to go in and pray. He knelt there before an image of Our Lord on His Cross and he felt great pleasure and consolation in his prayers so that his eyes were full of tears as he gazed at the Cross. Then, with his own ears, he heard a miraculous voice coming to him from the Cross, saying three times, "Francis, go and repair my house. You see, it is all falling down." At first he was terrified at the divine command expressed in these extraordinary words; but then he was filled with joy and wonder, and he stood up immediately prepared to put his whole heart into obeying the command and repairing the material building. However, the message really referred to

the Universal Church which Christ bought with the price of His Precious Blood, as the Holy Spirit afterwards made him realize, and he himself explained to his close companions. (*The Minor Life*, Chapter 1, Lesson 5)

St. Bonaventure describes that the Holy Spirit directed St. Francis into the little chapel of St. Damian's, for this encounter in prayer with Christ Crucified. Later on, the Holy Spirit gradually enlightened St. Francis as to the true spiritual nature of the mission Jesus gave him to repair the Church. His efforts were to be directed, not so much at rebuilding chapels of mortar and stone, like the dilapidated San Damiano, but at "rebuilding" the Church or dwelling place of God in the hearts of His people. The people's faith had grown weak, their love for God had grown cold. Our Lord commissioned St. Francis to stir up these virtues once again by the good example of his life, the power of his preaching, and the influence of his spiritual sons and daughters in the Franciscan family.

On another occasion St. Francis heard the Gospel story in which Christ sent the Apostles out, commanding them to take neither money nor provisions for their journey. He also commanded them to preach the Good News of salvation to the people. Francis felt that this is precisely what Jesus wanted him to do as well. He began to go about preaching to the people. Through the power and inspiration of the Holy Spirit, his preaching was greatly effective:

> Like a second Elias, Francis now began to take up the defense of truth, all inflamed as he was with the fiery ardor of the Spirit of Christ. He invited others to join him in the pursuit of perfect holiness urging them to lead a life of penance. His words were full of the power of the Holy Spirit, never empty or ridiculous, and they went straight to the depths of the heart, so that his hearers were astonished beyond measure and hardened sinners were moved by their penetrating power. (*The Minor Life*, Chapter 2, Lesson 2)

St. Bonaventure further wrote that Francis enjoyed the consolation of the Holy Spirit when he received the first of his followers, a young man from Assisi named Bernard of Quintavalle.

As the force of Francis' teaching and the sincerity of his life became known, others were moved by his example to live a life of penance. They renounced everything they had and came to share his life and dress. First among them was Bernard, a worthy man who was called by God and became Francis' first son, both in time and holiness. When he had discovered Francis' holiness for himself, he decided to renounce the world completely after his example, and he asked his advice about the best way to do it. Francis was filled with the encouragement of the Holy Spirit when he realized he was being joined by his first follower. (*The Major Life*, Chapter 3, Paragraph 3)

A final example of St. Francis' experience of the Holy Spirit occurred shortly after he had received his first seven followers. Francis had gone to a hermitage to pray, especially to express sorrow to God over the sins of his youth. There he received a further consolation of the Holy Spirit that his sins had been forgiven.

One day when he was in a lonely place by himself, weeping for his misspent years in the bitterness of his heart, the joy of the Holy Spirit was infused into him and he was assured that all his sins had been forgiven. (*The Major Life*, Chapter 3, Paragraph 6)

These examples serve to illustrate two important points. First, they show how aware St. Francis was of the presence of the Holy Spirit in his personal life. Secondly, they show us how open he was to following the lead of the Spirit, treasuring this precious Gift of God. These examples from the life of St. Francis should encourage us to pray for a greater awareness and openness to the Holy Spirit, in order to experience His working in our own daily lives.

Footnotes

1. This reminds me of the admonition of St. Paul to young Timothy:

   For this reason, I remind you to stir into flame the Gift of God bestowed when my hands were laid on you. The Spirit God has given us is no cowardly Spirit but rather one that makes us strong, loving, and wise. (2 Timothy 1:6-7)

2. St. Bonaventure actually wrote two accounts of his life. The first, entitled *The Minor Life*, was written for the friars to use for meditating on the life of their saintly founder; the second, entitled *The Major Life*, was written for the general public. In his two accounts, St. Bonaventure frequently told of the working of the Holy Spirit in the life of Francis; in fact, there are over sixty references to the Holy Spirit in *The Major Life* alone.

Chapter 4

Decline in Devotion to the Holy Spirit

A NYONE FAMILIAR WITH CHURCH history knows that if there have been good days, then there have also been bad days in the life of the Church. There have been, as we have just seen, individuals as well as times and movements when devotion to the Holy Spirit flourished; but there have also been times of decline. Some of this decline resulted from denial of the true identity of the Holy Spirit, while other aspects of decline have been due to exaggerations or distortions of devotion to Him.

DENIAL OF THE DIVINITY OF THE HOLY SPIRIT

Without doubt, the worst days in Church history regarding the understanding of the Holy Spirit and devotion to Him were the days of the so-called Macedonian heresy.

The Macedonian Heresy

This heresy, in the later half of the fourth century, denied the divinity of the Holy Spirit. It held that He was neither God nor the Third Person of the Blessed Trinity. It is useful for us to briefly examine the background to this heresy. This will also help us better appreciate the authentic teaching of the Church on the Holy Spirit.

Actually, another heresy, called Arianism, prepared the way

for the Macedonian heresy. At the beginning of the fourth century, a priest by the name of Arius from Alexandria in Egypt, denied the divinity of Jesus, saying that He was neither the Son of God nor the Second Person of the Blessed Trinity. Arius claimed that Jesus had a beginning (and therefore He could not be God because God is from all eternity). Instead, Arius said that Jesus Christ was simply an intermediary creature between God and the world. In 325 A.D., the Council of Nicea, the First Ecumenical Council of the Church, forcefully condemned Arius' teaching as heresy.

Sometime later, after the middle of the fourth century, the then Bishop of Constantinople, Macedonius, was accused of teaching the heresy which to this day bears his name. Just as Arius had denied the divinity of Jesus, the Son of God, Macedonius denied the divinity of the Holy Spirit. Those who followed the Macedonian heresy believed that the Holy Spirit was only a creature, not God, not divine, not the Third Person of the Blessed Trinity. Those who held this heresy became known popularly by the Greek word, "Pneumatomachoi" (literally, the "enemies" or "opponents" of the Spirit). In 381 A.D. at Constantinople, the Second Ecumenical Council in the Church officially condemned Macedonianism as a heresy.

In 382 A.D., Pope Damasus ratified the decisions of this Ecumenical Council. Its teaching was then added to the Creed that had earlier been formulated at the Council of Nicea in 325 A.D. It expressed a strong emphasis on the divinity of the Holy Spirit.[1] What the First Council of Constantinople defended and taught about the Holy Spirit is summarized in these words from the "Nicene Creed":

> We believe in the Holy Spirit, the Lord, the Giver of Life, Who proceeds from the Father and the Son. With the Father and the Son He is worshipped and glorified. He has spoken through the prophets.

This brief statement on the Holy Spirit very clearly and emphatically expresses our belief in His divinity. The Holy Spirit is called "Lord"; this is a divine title. Furthermore, He is referred to as the "Giver of life," and all life, as we know, ultimately comes from God. It is said that He "proceeds from the Father and the Son" because He is the bond of Their mutual love in the life of the Blessed Trinity. The Creed also stresses that with the Father and the Son He is "worshipped and glorified." This was the Council's way of saying that He is equal to the Father and to the Son Who are both acknowledged to be Divine Persons. Therefore, He is equal with Them to the point of being worshipped and praised as They are. This is again another way of saying that He is a Divine Person. Finally, there is a reference to the fact that He has "spoken through the prophets," because we see the working of the Spirit even in Old Testament times accomplishing God's work among His people.

DISTORTION OF DEVOTION TO THE HOLY SPIRIT

In addition to a denial of the divinity of the Holy Spirit, decline in true devotion to the Spirit has also come about either as a result of abuses or in the form of exaggerated claims to possessing the Holy Spirit. There is in the history of religious experience what is referred to by the general catch-word, "enthusiasm."[2]

The Dangers of "Enthusiasm"

Among the characteristics of this "enthusiasm" is a desire to possess a more directly felt guidance of the Holy Spirit. This could easily lead a group or movement to see itself as "elitist," or "perfect," while at the same time having a disregard, if not a disdain, for those who are only "marginal Christians," weaker brothers and sisters who plod and stumble on the religious path of life.

A good example of this phenomenon is the attitude of a group in the early centuries of Christianity who were referred to as "Gnostics" (from the Greek word, "gnosis," meaning knowledge). They claimed to possess a very special or superior or "enlightened" knowledge of religious mysteries that other "ordinary" or "unenlightened" believers did not possess.[3]

Joachimism

Another example of an "enthusiastic movement" in Church history is "Joachimism," named after an Italian mystic, Joachim of Fiore (c. 1130-1202). While on a pilgrimage to the Holy Land, he was converted from a worldly life. As a result, he entered a Cistercian abbey, was ordained a priest and later was elected abbot. In time he resigned his office to devote himself to writing. Afterward, he founded a reform abbey of strict observance at Fiore in Calabria. His contemporaries regarded him as a holy man and an eloquent preacher.

What is of interest to us is Joachim's idea of history. Writing books based on a mystical interpretation of the Book of Revelation, he introduced a kind of "theology of history" in which he saw salvation history as divided into three ages or periods, each one corresponding to One of the Three Divine Persons of the Blessed Trinity.

The first period was "the Age of the Father," in which God the Father ruled with power. It was an age characterized by fear and servile obedience. It corresponded to the Old Testament period in which the Father ruled by the harsh dispensation of the Old Testament Law. This first age eventually moved into the second.

The second period was "the Age of the Son," in which God the Son ruled through wisdom. It was an age characterized by faith, grace and filial obedience. During this age, the "Petrine" (from St. Peter) or visible or hierarchical Catholic Church was established. This age corresponded to the New Testament period. Joachim, however, taught that this age would pass into a third age.

The third period was "the Age of the Holy Spirit." Joachim announced that this age would begin relatively soon, sometime around 1260. According to Joachim, the reign of the Spirit would be characterized by universal love and liberty. This universal love would proceed from the Gospel of Jesus, not from its letter, but from its spiritual interpretation. Accordingly, the "Petrine" or visible Catholic Church would be absorbed into an invisible spiritual Church, the "Johannine" Church (from St. John the Beloved, author of the Book of Revelation). During this age, the "Eternal Gospel"[4] would be announced. It would be a time of great signs and idyllic conditions. For example, there would be a great conversion of the Jews; the Orthodox Churches and the Catholic Church would be reunited; all wars would cease.

In 1215, the Fourth Lateran (Ecumenical) Council condemned Joachim's teachings as heresy. Although Joachim had emphasized the Holy Spirit, he had done so at the cost of ignoring the Father and the Son. He became guilty of a heretical Trinitarian teaching called "Tritheism" (literally, "three Gods"). Tritheism holds that there are not only Three Divine Persons in God, but Three Divine Natures as well. This is the equivalent of saying that there are three Gods, not one God. Joachim did not distinguish between nature and person in God. He concluded that because there are Three Persons in God, there must be Three Natures. Joachim's teaching, however, destroyed the unity of God's nature as one God.

In regard to his "theology of history," Joachim's teachings contained three other errors. First, he separated the Three Divine Persons as working alone in each of the three periods of history he recognized. This separation further destroyed the unity of the Blessed Trinity because all Three Divine Persons act together in regard to Their creatures. They act through Their nature, and Their nature is one. Second, because all Three Divine Persons possess the one and the same Divine Nature, They all possess the same divine qualities, namely, power, wisdom, and love. Joachim, however, distinguished them separately in each of the Three Divine Persons. He exclusively gave power to the Father, wisdom to the Son, and love to the Holy Spirit. Third, Joachim erred seriously in teaching that there were two distinct Churches, the "Petrine" (visible) and the "Johannine" (invisible). There is, always will be, and can only be one Church founded by Jesus and united by the Holy Spirit.[5]

Two other factors exacerbated Joachim's plight. First, some of his followers, who called themselves "Joachimists," further discredited Joachim's reputation by falsely publishing some of their own writings in his name. Second, despite the condemnation by the Fourth Lateran Council, Joachim's ideas were kept alive among a group of Franciscans known as the "Spirituals." These Spirituals tended to be extremely strict observers of the Rule and Testament of St. Francis, unfortunately even to the point of fanaticism. The Spirituals promoted Joachim's ideas because he had predicted that "the Age of the Holy Spirit" would be inaugurated by the coming of a great new "barefooted" order of contemplative men in the Church. The Spirituals saw themselves as this new order that Joachim had foretold. In 1256, Pope Alexander IV condemned some of their teachings, including a work entitled *The Introduction to the Eternal Gospel.* This book was an edition of Joachim's works which was regarded as the "Bible" of the coming Age of the Holy Spirit.

One important lesson we can learn from the mistakes of Joachimism is that devotion to the Holy Spirit must never exclude our love and devotion to both the Father and the Son. They must be united together. As we say in the Nicene Creed: "With the Father and the Son He (the Holy Spirit) is worshipped and glorified." In fact, when we pray to the Holy Spirit, He directs us to Jesus, and then in, with, and through Jesus He leads us to the Father.

TENDENCIES TO AVOID IN DEVOTION TO THE HOLY SPIRIT

The exaggerations and distortions of "enthusiasm" can produce, and often have produced bizarre and unwelcomed consequences in regard to devotion to the Holy Spirit. Let us now look more closely at some of the dangerous tendencies of "enthusiasm," so as to avoid their negative effects in our own spiritual lives.

Danger of Emotionalism

Emotionalism is the first dangerous tendency to be avoided. Certain people seek a devotion to the Holy Spirit that is almost entirely "emotional." They seem to have a driven need to "feel" the presence of the Holy Spirit. In truth, however, we cannot "feel" God Himself, because God has no material makeup. Furthermore, because God is purely spiritual, our senses cannot have direct knowledge of Him. He does not touch them directly. What we "feel" is a certain "consolation" that God may allow us to experience so that by its unique "sweetness" and "joy," He may draw us closer to Himself.

Consolation, for example, can help us to pray especially when we are beginning to develop a prayer life. Beginners often need the joyful feeling of consolation to help them to pray more fervently until they learn how to pray more faithfully. In other words, beginners in the spiritual life tend to pray more from feelings than from faith. That can be helpful. But danger comes if people seek this "consoling feeling" or "sweetness" as the main goal of their spiritual efforts rather than learning to focus on their relationship with the Lord. St. John of the Cross summed up this tendency in a famous quote, "We must seek the God of consolations and not simply the consolations of God."

In summary, we realize that sometimes the working of the Holy Spirit is accompanied by strong feelings of fervor or consolation. On the other hand, it may be accompanied by no feelings at all; in fact, a person may experience dryness and even spiritual darkness. In either case, the authentic working of the Holy Spirit can only be known through the results or "fruits" that His graces produce in our lives. It would certainly hinder our spiritual growth and it might even do serious harm to our spiritual life if we were to insist on enjoying emotional consolations or "feelings" of the presence of the Holy Spirit, rather than on being open to His presence and His Will for us, even if it means dryness or emptiness of feelings.

Danger of Pride

A second dangerous tendency to avoid in our devotion to the Holy Spirit is the feeling of pride. This can easily overcome a person who has received various gifts of the Holy Spirit. This was a situation that plagued St. Paul in his relationship to the Church community in Corinth. In his First Letter to the Corinthians, St. Paul made frequent mention of the Holy Spirit and His gifts. Because they seemed to possess these gifts in abundance, many of the Corinthians became rather proud; they began to look down on those who did not possess the same gifts. St. Paul wrote to challenge them on this very point:

> Who confers any distinction on you? What do you possess that you have not received? But if you have received it, why are you boasting as if you did not receive it? (1 Corinthians 4:7)

The danger of pride is always present in the spiritual life. A humble person is clearly aware that every gift he or she possesses has been given by God. Accordingly, we must use them not for our own vainglory, but rather for the good of others as well as for our own growth in holiness. The Spirit's gifts are essential for carrying out God's Will in our daily lives.

A feeling of pride, however, often puffs up a person with an exaggerated sense of his or her own self-importance and can easily lead to self-righteous attitudes of being better-than-thou: "I received the gifts of the Spirit and you did not!" or "I'm a 'first-class' Christian, while you are definitely 'second class'!"[6]

St. Paul told the Corinthians that the way which matters most is not the way of the gifts, but rather the way of charity. We read further on in that same letter:

> Set your hearts on the greater gifts. Now I will show you the way which surpasses all the others. If I speak with human tongues and angelic as well, but do not have love, I am a noisy gong, a clanging cymbal. If I have the gift of prophecy and with full knowledge comprehend all mysteries, if I have faith great enough to move mountains but have not love, I am

nothing. If I give everything I have to feed the poor and hand over my body to be burned but have not love, I gain nothing. (1 Corinthians 12:31, 13:1-3)

Ultimately, we will all be judged by God not on how many gifts we have received but on how much we have loved Him and on how faithfully we have striven to carry out His Will. Our Lord Himself taught this point very clearly in the Sermon on the Mount.

You can tell a tree by its fruit. None of those who cry out "Lord, Lord" will enter the kingdom of God, but only the one who does the Will of My Father in heaven. When that day comes, many will plead with Me, "Lord, Lord, have we not prophesied in Your name? Have we not exorcised demons by its power? Did we not do many miracles in Your name as well?" Then I will declare to them solemnly, "I never knew you. Out of My sight, you evildoers!" (Matthew 7:20-23)

God's gifts, both physical and spiritual, are given to us so that we might use them to promote God's glory, to grow in holiness, to help us spread the Kingdom of God, and to assist our brothers and sisters in their physical and spiritual needs. We must never let the gifts that the Holy Spirit has given us or the deeds He has accomplished in and through us ever become opportunities for our own pride, vanity, or boasting. Rather, we must grow in the virtue of humility and learn to give over to God the glory that is His from the Spirit's working in us.

Danger of Rejecting the Church

A third dangerous tendency of exaggerated devotion to the Holy Spirit is the tendency to feel so "free" in the Spirit that one rejects all need for the Church. This is the attitude of those persons who reject the Church's teaching and doctrine, feeling that they are internally "enlightened" or "led" by the Holy Spirit Himself. This same tendency is also seen in the rejection of the leadership and guidance of the Catholic Church that Christ has established.

There have been in the course of history many enthusiastic movements that have appealed to what is called an "inner light" Church. Adherents of these movements often claim some direct illumination and guidance of the Holy Spirit, thereby eliminating any need for Church authority. For example, as we have seen in Joachimism, the "visible" or hierarchical Church in "the Age of the Son" became an "invisible" or inner spiritual Church in "the Age of the Holy Spirit." Yet Christ said clearly of His disciples:

> He who hears you, hears Me. He who rejects you, rejects Me. And he who rejects Me, rejects Him Who sent Me. (Luke 10:16)

These disciples spoke with the authority of Christ. Today, the pope and bishops, having the responsibility to teach and guide the people of God in the Church, speak with a similar authority from Christ.

This third tendency further shows itself in the rejection of the various Sacraments. Sometimes a person may mistakenly feel, "I have the Holy Spirit, I don't need any other means of grace such as the Sacraments." Yet, the Lord would never contradict His own revealed teaching. He would neither deny nor contradict the very authority He set up to guide His Church and to teach His people in His own Name, and to sanctify them by the administration of the Sacraments He instituted.

The Holy Spirit's interior working in our soul does not eliminate the place of the Scriptures, nor the teaching authority, nor the Sacraments that Christ gave to His Church. In fact, the Spirit's hidden, unseen mission within us uses and builds upon what we have already gained through these external gifts with which Christ has richly endowed His Church. It would certainly be an exaggeration and distortion of our devotion to the Holy Spirit to assume that His presence within us renders all other aspects of our Catholic Faith unnecessary. This would be a contradiction of Christ's own intention for His Church, and we can be sure that the Holy Spirit would not be a part of such a contradiction.

Decline in Devotion to the Holy Spirit

* * * * *

In this chapter and the previous one, we have looked in a very general way at various aspects of fervor and decline in regard to devotion to the Holy Spirit. From the examples of those individuals who have been fervent, may we be encouraged to know, love, and listen more faithfully to the Holy Spirit in our daily lives. On the other hand, we must also learn to avoid the mistakes and exaggerations of those movements, individuals and tendencies that have brought about the decline. We must always remember that sound devotion requires a sound theological basis. Authentic holiness can and must spring only from a solid foundation rooted in the truth of our Catholic Faith.

Footnotes

1. Catholics make a special profession of their Faith in the Three Divine Persons of the Blessed Trinity every Sunday and on Solemnities when they profess at Mass the Creed that has come down to them, combining the teachings of the first two Ecumenical Councils of the Church, Nicea and Constantinople. In fact, this is why the full proper name of the Creed is the "Nicene-Constantinopolitan Creed"; however, it is popularly known simply as the "Nicene Creed."
2. Our English word comes from a Greek word meaning literally "God within us." (The ancient Greeks felt that if a person was "enthusiastic," it was a spark of God's life within them that caused this joyful excitement.) The word "enthusiasm" as used here has a more technical meaning. According to Fr. Ronald Knox (who wrote a book entitled *"Enthusiasm,"* dealing with this particular phenomenon), it refers not so much to a special movement as to a tendency in many movements. According to him, it is a recurring phenomenon in Church history.
3. In his book *"Enthusiasm,"* Fr. Knox describes this tendency as "ultra supernaturalism."
4. "Eternal Gospel" is a reference to Revelation 14:6, where we read:

    > Then I saw another angel flying in mid-heaven, the herald of everlasting good news (Eternal Gospel) to the whole world, to every nation, race, language, and people.

5. Joachim had actually submitted his writings to the judgment of the Church, but he died before any judgment could be given. In fact, his writings were not condemned as heretical until years after his death.
6. This reminds me of the saying on a little humorous identification card for Catholics which reads, "I am an outstanding Catholic; in case of an accident, call a Bishop or at least a Monsignor."

II.

THE HOLY SPIRIT: THE SPIRIT OF LIFE

Chapter 5

The Spirit of Life

S OME OF THE GREATEST art masterpieces in the world are painted
on the ceiling and walls of the Sistine Chapel in Vatican City.
They are the fruits of the artistic genius of Michelangelo. Among the
paintings is the famous portrayal of the creation of man. Through
means of striking contrasts, the painting portrays God the Father as
Creator and Adam as creature. God the Father, in divine majesty,
reaches out His all powerful creative hand and gives life to Adam.
Adam, reaching with a dignity reflecting someone made in the
image and likeness of God, displays a certain weakness and frailty.
The finger of the Father's right hand touches the finger of Adam's
left hand. The Father's finger is firm and strong; Adam's is drooping
and weak. The Father's finger is life-giving; Adam's is life-receiv-
ing.

The life-giving finger of the Father's right hand is really a
symbol of the Holy Spirit. It represents the Spirit's presence and
power in the work of creation. The traditional Latin hymn in honor
of the Holy Spirit, "Veni, Creator, Spiritus" ("Come, Creator,
Spirit"), dating from the 9th century, clearly expresses this symbol
of the Holy Spirit as the "Digitus Paternae Dextrae" (literally, "The
Finger of the Father's Right Hand"). To quote the first three stanzas
of this inspiring hymn:

> Come, Creator, Spirit
> visit the souls of Your own;

fill with heavenly grace
the breasts that You have created.

You Who are called Paraclete,
Gift of the Most High God,
living water, flame, charity
and spiritual anointing.

You Who are sevenfold in Your gift,
Finger of God's right hand,
You Who were rightly promised by the Father,
enrich our throats with speech.

Every Sunday and Solemnity we proclaim in the Nicene Creed at Mass: "We believe in the Holy Spirit, the Lord, the Giver of Life." It is therefore fitting that we focus on life as the first manifestation of God Himself. He alone is the Source of all life. He possesses it as His own in an absolute way. He does not so much HAVE life, rather, He IS life! All other living things draw their life from His. Life is the first and most basic reality upon which all other realities rest; it is the gift that contains all other gifts!

THE LIFE-GIVING SPIRIT

It is theologically important to state that all Three Divine Persons of the Blessed Trinity together give us life. The reason for this is because They always act together in unison when dealing with the people and things They have created. This chapter, however, focuses specifically on the special life-giving mission and power of the Holy Spirit.

The Holy Spirit is life-giving in four instances. Two deal with creation: the FIRST creation and the NEW creation; the other two deal with death and life: JESUS' and OURS. In this chapter we shall look at the life-giving Spirit in creation and in Jesus' death and life; in the following chapter, we shall examine His role in our own death and life.

The Spirit of Life

The First Creation

The FIRST creation took place at the beginning of time. It was the creation of all things that God called forth into existence, none of which had yet existed. Only God Himself previously existed. It was God's almighty power alone that created something out of nothing. The Spirit of Life was at work in this FIRST creation. The opening lines of Genesis contain the first mention of the Spirit.[1]

> In the beginning, when God created the heavens and earth, the earth was a formless wasteland, and darkness covered the abyss, while a mighty wind swept over the waters.(Genesis 1:1-2)

A footnote to the New American Bible translation indicates that "mighty wind" literally can be read in the original Hebrew as either "a wind of God" or "a spirit of God." The reason for this is because the same Hebrew word, "ruah," can be translated as either "spirit" or "wind" or even "breath."

Thus, in the beginning God created the earth devoid of any form, beauty, or life. Likewise, there existed the "abyss," a kind of primitive watery deep covered with "darkness." Over this emptiness and dark abyss the Holy Spirit — like a mighty wind — moved. His "sweeping" over them eventually brought forth form, beauty, and, above all, life!

In the following days of the creation account in Genesis, all creation comes alive! The seas are filled with fish and living creatures of all kinds, the land abounds in vegetation, and animals of all species inhabit the land. Finally, there is the creation of the first man and woman, the highest expression of God's creative power and love. God Himself looks at all that He has created and finds them "very good" (Genesis 1:31).

It was the overshadowing of the Holy Spirit at the first moment of the Old Testament that empowered the FIRST creation to break forth into life. Wonderful as this First Creation was, however, the Spirit of Life brought about an even greater New Creation.

The New Creation

This NEW creation took place in the fullness of time. It was the moment of the Incarnation when God joined Himself to His own creation: the Son of God became incarnate and became the Son of the Virgin Mary.[2] St. Paul described the impact of the New Creation:

> When the designated time had come, God sent forth His Son born of a woman, born under the Law, to deliver from the Law those who were subjected to it, so that we might receive our status as adopted sons. (Galatians 4:4-5)

In the Prologue of his Gospel, St. John also proclaimed this greatest moment in human history in the context of a NEW creation. He used words reminiscent of the introduction in Genesis to the account of the FIRST creation: "In the beginning . . ."

> In the beginning was the Word; the Word was in God's presence, and the Word was God . . . (John 1:1)

Then, he proclaimed another and even greater "creative" act of God's mercy and love for us:

> The Word became flesh and made His dwelling among us, and we have seen His glory, the glory of an only Son coming from the Father, filled with enduring love. (John 1:14)

It was the Holy Spirit Who was present again to bring about this great Mystery of Life and Love. In contrast to the Spirit's "sweeping over" the formless earth and dark abyss at the FIRST creation to bring forth life, the Holy Spirit "overshadowed" the Virgin Mary of Nazareth at the Annunciation. In response to the Archangel Gabriel's announcement that she had been chosen by God and that she would bear a Son, Mary asked:

> "How can this be since I do not know man?" The angel answered her: "The Holy Spirit will come upon you and the power of the Most High will overshadow you; hence the holy offspring to be born will be called Son of God." (Luke 1:34-35)

Precisely at that moment the Incarnation, the highest point of all God's creative work in the universe, occurred:

> The Word became flesh and made His dwelling among us.
> (John 1:14)

Jesus, Who proclaimed that He had come precisely to give us life in all its fullness (John 10:10), was conceived in the womb of the Virgin Mary through the power of the Holy Spirit. We solemnly proclaim this fact as a truth of our Catholic Faith in the Nicene Creed: "By the power of the Holy Spirit He was born of the Virgin Mary, and became Man. . ."

St. Joseph was one of the first persons to whom this mystery of the Incarnation as the life-giving work of the Holy Spirit was revealed:

> Joseph, Son of David, have no fear about taking Mary as your wife. It is by the Holy Spirit that she has conceived this Child. She is to have a Son and you are to name Him Jesus because He will save His people from their sins. (Matthew 1:20-21)

In imitation of the faith, love, and trusting obedience of St. Joseph, we, too, must be ready to receive Jesus as the Word Incarnate, the Son of God and the Son of Mary, into our own midst.

Jesus' Death and Life

The third manifestation of the Spirit of Life took place when Jesus experienced His "Paschal Mystery," namely, at His Death, His Resurrection, and His Glorification.[3] We can actually distinguish three bestowals of the Holy Spirit, which occurred, respectively, on Good Friday, Easter Sunday, and Pentecost Sunday. These bestowals initiated the new life of the Church. The Holy Spirit became the "Soul" or inner source of life in the Mystical Body of Christ, the Church.

In his Gospel, St. John tells us that the Holy Spirit would only be given when Jesus was glorified (John 7:39). Our Lord confirmed this at the Last Supper when He told His Apostles:

> I tell you the sober truth: It is much better for you that I go. If
> I fail to go, the Paraclete will never come to you; whereas if I
> go, I will send Him to you. (John 16:7)

The reason for the Lord's statement was clear: The Paraclete, the Holy Spirit, would continue — albeit in a hidden, interior way — the spiritual formation of the Apostles which Our Lord had visibly commenced. Jesus' departure constituted His "Paschal Mystery," His glorious return to the Father. It consisted of His saving Death, His triumphant Resurrection, and His Ascension to His place of glory at the right hand of the Father united with His sending of the Holy Spirit at Pentecost as He had promised. In each instance there was a pouring forth of the Spirit of Life.

The Spirit Is Given Initially at Calvary

Prior to His death Our Lord taught the Apostles by way of different images which linked suffering and death with new life. He had told them how a grain of wheat must fall into the ground and die; but once it dies, it will give abundant new life (John 12:24).[4] He also used the image of a woman about to give birth. When she is in labor, she is in pain and sorrow; but once she gives birth, she no longer remembers the suffering because of the joy she has in the child born to her (John 16:21).[5] Note that in both these images suffering or death precede joy or life.

In a similar way, Jesus' death on Calvary resulted in a new life. This new life was the life of the Church beginning to emerge mysteriously. Jesus is dying; the Church is coming to life. This can be seen symbolized in the blood and water which flowed from the side of Our Lord when He was pierced on the cross by the centurion's spear:

> One of the soldiers thrust a lance into His side, and immedi-
> ately blood and water flowed out. (This testimony has been
> given by an eyewitness, and his testimony is true. He tells what
> he knows is true, so that you may believe.) (John 19:34-35)

The blood and water symbolically represent the Church. They stand for the Sacraments of the Eucharist and Baptism respectively.[6]

Indeed, the formation of the Church at Calvary was a favorite theme of the early Church Fathers. For example, St. John Chrysostom, a bishop in the fourth century, wrote in one of his catecheses:

> "There flowed from His side water and blood." Beloved, do not pass over this mystery without thought; it has yet another hidden meaning, which I will explain to you. I said that water and blood symbolized Baptism and the Holy Eucharist. From these two sacraments the Church is born: from Baptism, the cleansing water that gives rebirth and renewal through the Holy Spirit, and from the Holy Eucharist. Since the symbols of Baptism and the Eucharist flowed from His side, it was from His side that Christ fashioned the Church, as He had fashioned Eve from the side of Adam . . . Moses gives a hint of this when he tells the story of the first man and makes him exclaim: "Bone from my bones and flesh from my flesh." As God then took a rib from Adam's side to fashion a woman, so Christ has given us blood and water from His side to fashion the Church. God took the rib when Adam was in a deep sleep, and in the same way Christ gave us the blood and the water after His own death. (*The Catecheses* of St. John Chrysostom, Cat. 3, 13-19; SC 50, 174-77 in the *The Liturgy of the Hours*, Vol. II, pp. 472-73)

Jesus' death, then, is like a "new birth" giving life to the Church. It is precisely at this very moment that the Spirit of Life is referred to as being present. St. John indicated this in the account of Our Lord's death:

> Jesus, realizing that everything was now finished, said to fulfill the Scripture: "I am thirsty." There was a jar there, full of common wine. They stuck a sponge soaked in this wine on some hyssop and raised it to His lips. When Jesus took the wine, He said, "Now it is finished." Then He bowed His head and delivered over His spirit. (John 19:28-30)

This reference to Jesus "delivering over His spirit" has a double meaning in the original Greek. On the one hand, it refers to Jesus Who, in the act of dying, surrendered His very last breath as a sign of His complete submission to His Heavenly Father's Will.[7] In this sense, St. Luke preserved one of the seven last words of Our Lord on the Cross:

Father, into Your Hands I commend My spirit. (Luke 23:46)

On the other hand, Jesus' "delivering over His spirit" also seems to refer to His conferring of the Holy Spirit upon the Church. As set forth above, the Church is symbolically seen as being "born" from Jesus' side when the blood and water flow from His pierced Heart. Because the Church was beginning to come alive, the Spirit of Life had to be present. At the very moment of His death, Jesus began to pour forth His promised Spirit of Life. This was the first time Jesus conferred the Life-Giving Spirit on His people. Had He not told those who thirsted for eternal life to come to Him, and He would create in them rivers of living water? As St. John comments:

Here He was referring to the Spirit, Whom those that came to believe in Him were to receive. There was, of course, no Spirit as yet, since Jesus had not yet been glorified. (John 7:39)

Jesus' death on the Cross on Good Friday was the very beginning of His glorification — He was now returning to His place of glory in Heaven at the right hand of His Father. It was also the beginning of His conferring of the Spirit of Life on His disciples because He was now being glorified.

The Spirit Is Given Uniquely to the Apostles on Easter Sunday

Our Lord won for us the Gift of God, the Holy Spirit, by His saving death. Now by His Easter Resurrection He further bestowed on His Church the Holy Spirit with His life-giving mission.

St. John tells us that Our Risen Lord appeared to His Apostles on Easter night. He greeted them with His peace and showed them

His pierced hands and side to reassure them He had truly risen. Then, ready to send them forth as His Apostles ("apostle" is from the Greek word meaning "one who is sent"), the Holy Spirit was given to them:

> "Peace be with you," He said again. "As the Father has sent Me, so I send You." Then He breathed on them and said, "Receive the Holy Spirit. If you forgive men's sins, they are forgiven them; if you hold them bound, they are held bound." (John 20:21-23)

Again, the Holy Spirit is here referred to in His life-giving mission. He is given to the Apostles so that they themselves may have eternal life. The Apostles received the Holy Spirit, Who was breathed on them in much the same way that God had breathed the breath of life into Adam (Genesis 2:7).

But the Spirit of Life is also given so that the Apostles can share His life-giving mission with others among God's people. The Holy Spirit has the mission of "sanctifying us." This means, first of all, that He frees us from our sins that keep us from God. He then makes us "just" and pleasing to God, filling us with the Sanctifying Grace of Eternal Life (changing us from sinners to saints, from God's enemies to His friends).

When the Apostles received the Holy Spirit they were cleansed of all their personal sins. At the same time, they were given the power of the Holy Spirit to take away the sins of the People of God in Jesus' Name: first, through Baptism, and second, through the great Sacrament of Reconciliation.

Approximately fifteen centuries later, the Council of Trent defined that the power Jesus conferred on Easter night to His Apostles to forgive sins is the same power priests exercise in Confession. Over the centuries, this power to forgive sins has been and still is a source of constant renewal and consolation for countless multitudes who continue to seek pardon and peace in this Sacrament of Peace.

I once heard it said, "A saint is nothing but a sinner who keeps trying." How renewing, refreshing, uplifting, and peaceful the Sacrament of Penance can prove to be. Despite the sins we repeatedly commit because of our weaknesses, it can make saints of us if we repent and keep trying again and again to live holy lives. It is as if the Holy Spirit is actually breathing fresh life into us! The Sacrament of Reconciliation is, in its own way, also a conferral of the Spirit of Life.

The Spirit Is Given Universally on Pentecost

The third time the Spirit of Life came in Jesus' Paschal Mystery was on Pentecost Sunday. After His Death and Resurrection, Our Lord ascended to Heaven to take up His place of glory at the right hand of His Heavenly Father. He had told the Apostles at the Last Supper that He was going away to prepare a place for His faithful servants in His Heavenly Kingdom. Furthermore, He would also await the moment for His return again in glory at the Parousia, at the time of the final judgment at the end of the world.

In the meantime, however, He promised to send us the Holy Spirit to carry on His mission among His followers throughout the centuries. He fulfilled this promise when He sent the Holy Spirit from the Father on Pentecost. At that moment, the Church, as God's New People, came to birth.

There were one hundred and twenty followers of Jesus gathered in the Upper Room on Pentecost (Acts 1:15). Jewish law required that number as a minimum for any new movement to be legally recognized. Furthermore, one tenth of that number also had to be in leadership roles; this legal requirement was met because there were twelve Apostles as leaders. In addition to the initial band of disciples, many others entered the Church that day. Pentecost would truly be the official "birthday" of the Church:

> Those who accepted his (St. Peter's) message were baptized; some three thousand were added that day. (Acts 2:41)

The Spirit of Life

Just as the human body needs the presence of the soul in it to be the source of life for all its activities, so too, the Church, which St. Paul called "the Body of Christ" (1 Corinthians 12:27), needs the presence of the Spirit of Life within it. He acts as the "Soul" of the Mystical Body of Christ, being the source of vitality for its growth and all its good works. The Spirit of Life will do this throughout the centuries, even to the very end of time.

Footnotes

1. As we read Genesis, we must keep one very important point in mind. In the Old Testament, the Mystery of the Blessed Trinity — our belief that in One God there are Three Divine Persons, the Father, the Son, and the Holy Spirit — had not yet been revealed. That revelation would take place later in the New Testament, with Jesus revealing His Heavenly Father as the First Divine Person; revealing Himself as the Son of God, the Second Divine Person; and promising to send us the Holy Spirit, the Third Divine Person.
   So when the Old Testament mentions the "spirit" of God, the Jewish people would not have understood this to mean a Divine Person. For them it would have meant a quality or "attribute" of God. They would have understood "spirit" to be the power of God by which He carried out all His works, whether creating the universe or forming a people in the desert at Mt. Sinai, whether moving some of the Israelites as prophets to preach God's message or inspiring others in the writing of the Old Testament Scriptures. In short, the "spirit" of God was the "power" of God guiding all the events in Israel's history that helped to prepare the way for the coming of Christ in the fullness of time. It is from our New Testament vantage point, with its fuller view of Revelation, that we can "look back" and understand the "spirit" or "power" of God in a fuller sense as a reference to the Third Divine Person, the Holy Spirit. We proclaim this also in the Nicene Creed: *We believe in the Holy Spirit . . . Who has spoken through the prophets.* These prophets had lived in the time of the Old Testament. In retrospect it is clearly understood that it was the Holy Spirit already at work among them!
2. This moment of the Incarnation divides all human history into two eras: B.C. (Before Christ) and A.D. ("Anno Domini" - "In the year of the Lord").
3. The Glorification of Jesus actually consisted of both His Ascension and His sending of the Holy Spirit. Because He ascended into His glory, He would send the Holy Spirit as the first Gift of His glorious victory over sin and death.
4. In reality, Our Lord Himself would be the first and greatest grain of the wheat to die, so that the abundant harvest of the world's salvation would soon follow!
5. This is a consistent point of contrast or paradox between life on the natural level and life on the supernatural level. In the natural life of our body, life precedes death and life leads to death; in the supernatural life of our soul, death precedes life and death leads to life.
6. In connection with this, it is helpful to recall that the Church is also symbolically presented as the mystical Spouse of Christ, "beautiful as a bride prepared to meet her husband" (Revelation 21:2). To understand and appreciate this symbolism, we must recall that St. Paul referred to Jesus as the "New Adam" (1 Corinthians 15: 45). It

logically would follow, then, that the Church, His mystical Spouse, can properly be called the "New Eve." Now, the first Eve was described in the creation account in Genesis as being formed from the side of the first Adam:

> So the Lord God cast a deep sleep on the man, and while he was asleep, He took out one of his ribs and closed up its place with flesh. The Lord God then built up into a woman the rib that He had taken from the man. (Genesis 2:21-22)

7. I remember hearing a very inspiring example of this final total surrender to God. It involved a very holy Capuchin-Franciscan priest (now up for canonization) who died in 1959. His name was Fr. Solanus Casey. He had always prayed to die while conscious. For about the last three days of his life, he was in a coma. Just moments before his death, he came out of the coma, sat up in bed and prayed aloud, "I give my soul to Jesus Christ." With that, his head fell back onto the pillow and he died. It was the final act of giving in a life that had been totally lived for God. Our Lord's words of self surrender would have had this same sense.

Chapter 6

The Spirit in Our Death and Life in Christ

IN THE PREVIOUS CHAPTER, we looked at three manifestations of the Spirit of Life in connection with Jesus' own death and life. Here we will reflect on the fourth manifestation of the Spirit of Life which is connected with our own personal sharing in Jesus' Paschal Mystery. This is seen primarily in our own Baptism and the new life it conferred on us; it can also be seen in the daily experience of living our Christian lives.

OUR DYING AND RISING IN BAPTISM

In the natural order of human life on earth, life precedes death. In contrast, in the supernatural order of the life we share with God through Sanctifying Grace, death precedes life and death leads to life. How true this is of our Baptism which is the very beginning of Christian life. It is a sharing, first in death, then in life. St. Paul emphasized this point to the first Christians of the Church in Rome:

> Are you not aware that we who were baptized into Christ Jesus were baptized into His death? Through baptism into His death we were buried with Him so that just as Christ was raised from the dead by the glory of the Father, we too might live a new life. If we have been united with Him through likeness to His death, so shall we be through a like resurrection. This we

know: our old self was crucified with Him so that the sinful body might be destroyed and we might be slaves to sin no longer. A man who is dead has been freed from sin. If we have died with Christ, we believe that we are also to live with Him. We know that Christ, once raised from the dead, will never die again; death has no more power over Him. His death was death to sin, once for all; His life is life for God. In the same way, you must consider yourselves dead to sin but alive for God in Christ Jesus. (Romans 6:3-11)

Baptism as Death with Jesus

In this passage, St. Paul clearly teaches that our Baptism is a dying experience. He does not mean that we die to our natural life in the body; after all, we can still breathe, talk, walk, eat, drink and so on. Rather, we die mysteriously or "supernaturally" to sin; our old sinful self is crucified and put to death, so to speak. Now, through the merits and power flowing from Jesus' Death and Resurrection, we can resist sin and its allurements. The dominant power that sin and our passions had over our lives — we were "slaves of sin" — is broken as we are joined with Jesus in His death on the Cross and His rising to new life. This new life is a life of Christian virtue in which we:

> put on the Lord Jesus Christ and make no provision for the desires of the flesh. (Romans 13:24)

The early Christians experienced this "new life" through the ordinary adult form of Baptism by immersion. It consisted of immersing a person three times into a body of water (e.g., a lake, a river, or a pool). The body of water represented the tomb and death. When the person was baptized, he was immersed or submerged into the water three times as the formula was said, "I baptize you in the Name of the Father (first immersion), and of the Son (second immersion), and of the Holy Spirit (third immersion)." Each time the person was submerged momentarily in the water, it symbolized his or her dying with Christ, being buried in the tomb with Him. This is why St. Paul asked the Christians at Rome whether they were aware that those who had been baptized into Christ Jesus were "baptized into His death" (Romans 6:3). In a mystical way, they had gone into the tomb with Jesus!

Baptism as Resurrection with Jesus

As the early Christians emerged from the water, they symbolically rose from death and from the tomb with Jesus. St. Paul wrote:

> If we have been united with Him through likeness to His death,
> so shall we be through a like resurrection. (Romans 6:5)

Our bodily resurrection has not yet occurred; that will take place on the last day when Jesus returns to judge the living and the dead. But we already now "live with Him" (Romans 6:8) through "Sanctifying Grace"; this constitutes the awesome presence of God in our souls that we call the "Divine Indwelling." We have become living tabernacles of God's presence in us.

The Scriptures teach very clearly that the Three Divine Persons dwell in us. Our Lord Himself at the Last Supper spoke of how He and His Heavenly Father dwell in the souls of those persons who love Him and live by His Commandments:

> Anyone who loves Me will be true to My word, and My Father
> will love him; We will come to him and make Our dwelling
> place with him. (John 14:23)

St. Paul wrote that the Holy Spirit also dwells in us because our bodies are His "temples":

> You must know that your body is a temple of the Holy Spirit
> Who is within — the Spirit you have received from God. You
> are not your own; you have been purchased, and at a price. So
> glorify God in your body. (1 Corinthians 6:19-20)

In a special way it is the mission of the Holy Spirit to guide us in our new life in Christ. He does so by the work of His gifts, the stirrings of His inspirations, and the growth of His love in our hearts.

Scripture abounds in evidence of the Holy Spirit's mission to be with us and assist us in the work of our sanctification. St. Paul frequently reminded the early Christians (and us, too) of this sublime mystery:

> The love of God has been poured out in our hearts through the Holy Spirit who has been given to us. (Romans 5:5)

> God (the Father) is the One Who firmly establishes us along with you in Christ; it is He Who anointed us and has sealed us, thereby depositing the first payment, the Spirit, in our hearts. (2 Corinthians 1:21-22)

OUR DAILY DYING TO SIN AND RISING TO MORE GENEROUS LOVE

Our dying and rising with Jesus began on the day of our Baptism, but it did not end there. It continues every day of our lives. St. John the Baptist summed up the Christian life when he said:

> He (Jesus) must increase, while I must decrease. (John 3:30)

What must decrease in us is the selfish, distorted love that resulted from the wound of Original Sin deep within us and which is further intensified by our daily personal sins. These sins pressure us to choose again and again our own self-centered concerns and desires to the exclusion of the just rights and expectations of God and the legitimate needs of our neighbor.

What must increase in us, however, is self-giving, Christ-like love. Our Lord described this perfect love in the two greatest of all the commandments: namely, to love God with our whole heart, soul, and mind, and to love our neighbor as ourselves (Matthew 22:37-38). In other words, there must be less self-centered love in our daily lives and more self-giving love. This is what the daily experience of dying and rising with Jesus is all about. This is an ongoing, daily process. St. Paul knew it well:

> Continually we carry about in our bodies the dying of Jesus,
> so that in our bodies the life of Jesus may also be revealed.

The Spirit in Our Death and Life in Christ

> While we live we are constantly being delivered to death for Jesus' sake, so that the life of Jesus may be revealed in our mortal flesh. (2 Corinthians 4:10-11)

THE HOLY SPIRIT DIRECTS OUR SPIRITUAL LIFE

It is the Spirit of Life Who, as the Director of the interior life within our souls, is continuously at work in us, bringing to completion the dying to our sinfulness and self-centeredness which began on the day of our Baptism. He will continue His work in us until we reach the fullness of the new life we have in Christ! This is the spiritual life, and the Holy Spirit has been given to us to bring it to completion for our sanctification. St. Paul summed this up well:

> If the Spirit of Him (the Father) Who raised Jesus from the dead dwells in you, then He who raised Christ from the dead will bring your mortal bodies to life also through His Spirit dwelling in you. We are debtors, then, my brothers — but not to the flesh, so that we should live according to the flesh. If you live according to the flesh, you will die; but if by the Spirit you put to death the evil deeds of the body, you will live. All who are led by the Spirit of God are sons of God. You did not receive a spirit of slavery leading you back into fear, but a spirit of adoption through which we cry out, "Abba" (that is "Father"). The Spirit Himself gives witness with our spirit that we are children of God. (Romans 8:11-16)

This Holy Spirit described by St. Paul is now the Giver of life for us, the source of our own personal spiritual life. As He made the universe life-giving at the time of creation, and as He made the womb of the Virgin Mary bring forth the incarnate life of the God-man, Jesus Christ, at the time of the Annunciation, so, too, the Holy Spirit brings forth in our own souls a mysterious sharing in the divine life of the Blessed Trinity. This new life we call "Sanctifying Grace." Accordingly, we say in the Nicene Creed: "We believe in the Holy Spirit, the Lord, the Giver of Life. . . ."

JESUS' TEACHING ON BAPTISM AND THE SPIRITUAL LIFE

Our Lord Himself stressed the need for a new spiritual life when He spoke to Nicodemus (John 3:1ff). Nicodemus was a Pharisee as well as a member of the ruling Jewish Council, the Sanhedrin. When he came to speak with Jesus, he already had the beginning of some faith in Him, for he tells Our Lord:

> We know you are a teacher come from God, for no man can perform signs and wonders such as You perform unless God is with him. (John 3:2)

New Birth and New Life

Sincerely seeking the truth, Nicodemus came to Jesus. However, he came under the cover of night because he did not want to be seen speaking to Jesus in public. Our Lord had probably already come under the suspicions of many of the Pharisees and Sadducees, and so Nicodemus did not want to risk being seen openly speaking with Him. Jesus responds to Nicodemus by saying:

> I solemnly assure you, no one can see the reign of God unless he is begotten from above. (John 3:3)

In this statement Jesus speaks of a new birth and with it new life. "To beget" someone is the role of a father in the act of conception, in the conceiving of new life. Our Lord here indicates that the way we enter the reign of God — the Kingdom of God — is through a new birth.

Our Lord tells us that we must be begotten "from above." This phrase, "from above," is extremely important. The Greek word for this phrase is "anothen." Actually in Greek "anothen" has two meanings. First, it can mean "again." If Jesus meant to be "begotten again," it would mean simply a second natural birth. Second, it could also mean "from above." This would indicate, not a second natural birth, but a different kind of birth, a spiritual birth from above, from Heaven. Nicodemus misunderstands the phrase to mean being born "again" by a second natural birth because he asks our Lord:

> How can a man be born again once he is old? Can he return to his mother's womb and be born over again? (John 3:4)

"Water" and "Spirit"

Nicodemus' question shows that he had misinterpreted Jesus' words. So Our Lord clarifies this point by saying:

> I solemnly assure you, no one can enter into God's Kingdom without being begotten of water and Spirit. (John 3: 5)

Here Our Lord describes what this new birth will be. It will be a birth that involves two things, one visible and the other invisible. Water is the visible part of this new birth through the Sacrament of Baptism, whether it is water poured on a person's forehead or water in which a person is totally immersed. This is the visible or outward sign of the Sacrament. But there is also an invisible part of this new birth by Baptism. This consists of being begotten of the Spirit. The pouring forth of the Holy Spirit invisibly into the heart of the person is what brings about the restoration of God's new life within, the life lost through Original Sin.

"Flesh" versus "Spirit"

Our Lord contrasts for Nicodemus two different kinds of life — a life that is rooted in the "flesh" and a life that is rooted in the Spirit. Our Lord tells Nicodemus:

> Flesh begets flesh, Spirit begets spirit. (John 3:6)

Our Lord compares two levels of life. The life indicated by the flesh means our fragile human life here on earth, that life which we received when we were born from our own mother's womb. This is a life which is weak, mortal, and passing away. Jesus does not say that this is the kind of life He wants to give us.

There is also the life of our spirit (soul). In contrast to the flesh, this interior life in the soul is strong, enduring, and immortal; it will not pass away because it is truly eternal life. Our Lord indicates to Nicodemus that through Baptism we receive the Holy Spirit, Who creates by His presence in our souls a new spiritual life, a life that will endure forever and will bring us ultimately to the Kingdom of Heaven.

The Reflections of St. Paul

This teaching of new life through the Holy Spirit is found elsewhere in the Scriptures. It was stressed frequently in the letters of St. Paul — as when, for example, he wrote to Titus, his young fellow-worker:

> He saved us through the baptism of new birth and renewal by the Holy Spirit. This Spirit He lavished on us through Jesus Christ Our Savior, that we might be justified by His grace and become heirs, in hope, of eternal life. You can depend on this to be true. (Titus 3:5-8)

THE SOUL'S MOST WELCOME GUEST

As set forth above, the Holy Spirit is clearly the "Giver of Life" because He comes to live in us as a result of our Baptism. We become His temples.[1] Although all Three Divine Persons dwell in us when we are in the state of Sanctifying Grace, the Fathers of the Church emphasized that this "Divine Indwelling" is the special characteristic of the Holy Spirit. This is why He has been given the beautiful title: "the soul's most welcome Guest"!

It is because of His dwelling within us that the Holy Spirit becomes the Source of continuous spiritual life in us. The Holy Spirit is the "Sanctifier"; He is in charge of the process of our growth in holiness. As part of His special work of sanctification — the process of making someone holy — He defends us from evil and inspires us to do good. He prepares us for the introduction to and the foretaste of the life of glory that all the saints in Heaven enjoy to the fullest.

Pope Leo XIII, in his famous encyclical letter on the Holy Spirit entitled *Divine Illud Munus* (1897), wrote:

> Through Baptism, the unclean spirit having been driven forth from the soul for the first time, the Holy Spirit enters into the soul and renders it like Himself.

Pope Leo XIII, by stating that the Holy Spirit "renders (the soul) like Himself," is telling us that the soul is transformed by the Divine Indwelling into the likeness of God Himself. Let us take the example of a piece of wood thrown into a fire. It can burn so intensely that at some point we can hardly distinguish the wood from the fire. The wood is so thoroughly saturated with the fire that it takes on the appearance of the fire. In a similar way, a soul possessing the Blessed Trinity within it takes on the beauty and the life of the Blessed Trinity. We do not become God Himself, in a pantheistic sense, like becoming a "Fourth Divine Person." Rather, we are transformed into the likeness of God so thoroughly that His divine image is impressed on the soul. Since this is the special work of the Holy Spirit, we speak of being "sealed" with the Holy Spirit. This means that the divine image of the Holy Spirit is impressed onto the soul, like a royal seal on wax. St. Paul mentions this "sealing" with the Holy Spirit:

> In Him (Jesus) you too were chosen: when you heard the glad tidings of salvation, the word of truth, and believed in it, you were sealed with the Holy Spirit Who had been promised. (Ephesians 1:13)

Sealed with the Holy Spirit

Some of the Fathers of the Church offered this explanation of the "sealing" by the Holy Spirit. They compared the soul of the person to liquid wax. The One Who impresses the "Seal" is the Holy

Spirit, and the "Seal" itself is also the Holy Spirit because the Holy Spirit is impressing Himself like a seal onto the soul. The soul, like wax, will receive His divine image. The Holy Spirit can give this likeness of Himself to the soul because He actually gives Himself. He is the Supreme Gift! He is the new Life of the soul, along with the Father and the Son.

There is an important detail in this explanation of the Fathers of the Church that we must keep in mind. They said that the soul is and always remains like liquid wax, at least during the whole lifetime of a person while he or she is on earth. In their explanation, since the liquid wax does not harden, the imprint in the wax will never be permanent by itself. It will always require the constant application of the "seal" to the wax for the image to remain. In a similar way, the "Seal" (the Holy Spirit) must be continuously applied to the soul or else His image or imprint on the soul will be lost.

This reminds us of a very important fact in the spiritual life. The Holy Spirit is the soul's most welcome Guest. However, a guest can remain only as long as he or she is invited and made to feel welcome. The Holy Spirit will never leave the soul on His own initiative. However, a person may indicate that the Holy Spirit is no longer welcome within his or her soul. This happens when the person commits a mortal sin. At that moment, the Holy Spirit, along with the Father and the Son, leave the soul. If the Spirit leaves the soul, His living divine image is lost from the soul.

The detail of the liquid wax reminds us, then, that the permanent presence of the Holy Spirit in the soul can never be taken for granted; we can lose it through mortal sin. Remember that Our Lord said at the Last Supper that He and the Father (and we must also include the Holy Spirit) would come to those who love Him and keep His word or His commandments (John 14:23). When we commit mortal sin, we are no longer loving God or keeping His word because mortal sin is a serious offense against God, His love, and His commandments. Such sin drives God's love from our hearts. It results in breaking the bond of love and friendship between the Blessed Trinity and the soul. Their divine presence in the soul ceases. So, too, the "Seal" of the Holy Spirit, imprinting His divine image onto the soul, withdraws. As the liquid wax becomes formless when the seal is withdrawn, the soul loses its share in the divine beauty and life. It becomes spiritually disfigured and spiritually dead.

"Mortal" means deadly, and mortal sin brings spiritual death to the soul. This helps us to understand why mortal sin is the worst of all possible evils. It alone can separate us from the Divine Indwelling in our souls, and it alone can deprive us of sharing in the divine life. It causes the life of God's grace within us to die. This is why the saints were resolved to renounce any possessions or pleasures, and to endure any sufferings or sacrifices, even to lose earthly life itself, rather than to commit a mortal sin. Their resolve was: "Death rather than (mortal) sin!"

We must safeguard the presence of the Spirit of Life in us by living our daily Christian life; this will allow us to remain in God's love by keeping His commandments. Then our soul will continuously draw life from the Divine Guest within us. We do well to pray for the Holy Spirit with the same prayer that the Church recites as a special sequence during the beautiful Mass for Pentecost. It is generally known by its Latin title, the "Veni, Sancte Spiritus" ("Come, Holy Spirit"). However, it is also called "The Golden Sequence" because of its great beauty, simplicity, and sweetness.

> Come, Holy Spirit, come!
> And from Thy celestial home
> Shed a ray of light divine!
>
> Come, Father of the poor!
> Come, Source of all our store!
> Come, within our bosoms shine!
>
> You, of Comforters the best;
> You, the soul's most welcome Guest;
> Sweet Refreshment here below;

In our labor, rest most sweet;
Grateful coolness in the heat;
Solace in the midst of woe.

O most blessed Light divine,
Shine within these hearts of Thine,
And our inmost being fill!

Where Thou art not, man has naught,
Nothing good in deed or thought,
Nothing free from taint of ill.

Heal our wounds, our strength renew;
On our dryness pour Thy dew;
Wash the stains of guilt away.

Bend the stubborn heart and will;
Melt the frozen, warm the chill;
Guide the steps that go astray.

On the faithful, who adore
And confess Thee evermore
In Thy sevenfold gift descend.

Give them virtue's sure reward;
Give them Thy salvation, Lord;
Give them joys that never end.

Amen. Alleluia.

Footnotes

1. Actually, as was pointed out, all Three Divine Persons of the Trinity, the Father, the Son, and the Holy Spirit, come to live in us. We referred to this divine presence in the soul as the Divine Indwelling through the gift we call Sanctifying Grace.

Chapter 7

Wind and Breath:
Symbols of the Spirit of Life

T HE BASIS OF OUR Catholic Faith is the belief that God has spoken
to His people by a special revelation. In the Judaeo-Christian
tradition, the Old and New Testaments, we believe that God has
revealed Himself and His message of love and salvation for the
world. When God tells us about Himself, we must keep in mind
some important facts. God, Who does the revealing, is eternal,
almighty, all-knowing, and infinitely perfect in every way. If He
were not, He would not be God. As a result, only God can totally and
perfectly know Himself. We cannot know Him perfectly because
we are not Divine Persons, but only human persons.

We who receive God's revelation are, in comparison to God
Himself, quite finite (limited) or imperfect (incomplete) in our
knowledge, power, and presence. So, God must speak to us in
human words and not in divine "language" or else we would not
understand Him. Yet, human words and ideas in and of themselves
cannot totally communicate to us Who God is, because human
words are finite or limited and God is not. Therefore, when God
speaks to us in human words, He speaks to us by way of what we call
an analogy.

An analogy is a comparison of two persons or ideas, one
known and the other unknown. In the comparison, the two persons
or ideas are seen to be partly the same and partly different. Insofar

as they are the same, we learn something; the difference continues to remain unknown to us. By an analogy, we come to know the unknown person (in our example, the Spirit of Life) by comparing Him to what we already know (e.g., water). Though an analogy cannot tell us everything about God (because nothing in our whole created world can ever perfectly be compared to God), it can tell us something, limited as it may be.

The word in the analogy serves as a symbol. A symbol is defined as: "something concrete that represents or suggests another thing that cannot in itself be represented or visualized."[1]

Let us look at a symbol of the Spirit of Life to illustrate the idea of analogy. When we say that water is a symbol of the Spirit of Life, we do not mean that He is some kind of liquid or that He has a chemical makeup of H_2O. Rather, we are saying that as all animals and plants need water to sustain their life processes, so we, too, need the Spirit of Life to sustain our Christian life. Furthermore, as water can be used for cleansing and purifying, so, too, when the Spirit of Life comes into our hearts, He purifies us of sin, as in our Baptism. He takes away the guilt of Original Sin. It is the same for the other symbols.

In order to understand more fully the connection between life and the Holy Spirit as its source, let us look at four things which were closely connected with life in the Sacred Scriptures and which are also in some way symbols of the Holy Spirit. As we reflect on each symbol, we will learn more about the Spirit of Life. In this chapter we will focus on the symbols of (1) Wind and (2) Breath. In the following chapter, we will focus on the symbols of (3) Water and (4) Fire.

WIND

The first two symbols, "wind" and breath," are closely linked to the Spirit of Life by the biblical Hebrew word "ruah." The ancient Jewish people used this same word to mean "wind" or "breath" or "spirit." This was because in biblical times these three realities were thought to be connected. The basic root of the word "ruah" means "air in motion," and this is the WIND. But it also can mean air inhaled and exhaled in respiration, and this is BREATH. Finally, the ancient Hebrews observed that when breathing stops, life also departs from inside the person. This led them to assume that there is also an inner source of life in the individual, a kind of "inner breath," and this is the human SPIRIT (soul).

For the ancient peoples "wind" had a certain element of mystery about it. It was inexplicable in terms of its origin, its movements, and its purpose. The wind was sometimes even spoken of as Yahweh's breath, as in the description of the parting of the waters of the Red Sea:

> At a breath of Your anger the waters piled up, the flowing
> waters stood like a mound, the flood waters congealed in the
> midst of the sea. (Exodus 15:8)

Three qualities of the wind help us in understanding the Holy Spirit: first, it is unpredictable; second, it is discernible; and third, it is forceful.

Free as the Wind

Lacking any scientific understanding, ancient peoples saw the wind as an unpredictable phenomenon. This gave the wind the characteristic of freedom of movement. (Even today we use the expression "as free as the wind.") Our Lord made this very point to Nicodemus:

> The wind blows where it will. You hear the sound it makes but
> you do not know where it comes from, or where it goes. So it
> is with everyone begotten of the Spirit. (John 3:8)

We learn from this analogy that the Holy Spirit's ways often seem mysterious and unpredictable. For example, who of us can be sure what God's providence will arrange in our lives for even just a day from now? Who of us can demand specific gifts of the Holy

Spirit or even a certain number of them when He simply distributes them as He wills (1 Corinthians 12:11)? We must respect the freedom of the Spirit in directing our lives. Our concern should be to be ready and willing to listen to His inspirations rather than ready to dictate our own prearranged agenda to Him.

Known By Its Effects

Yet, despite being unpredictable, the wind can be known in a certain way by its effects. The wind cannot be seen, but we can hear the noise it makes as it swirls around us, or we can observe its rustling of leaves or swaying of trees, or we can feel it blowing against us. In the same way, we cannot see the Holy Spirit, but we can know Him by His effects in us. To possess the Holy Spirit is to sense the beginning of a deep change in our lives. A real conversion emerges. The Spirit's presence is neither adequately nor accurately judged by our feelings and emotions. It can only be genuinely discerned by the fruits of His working in us.

Our Lord says that we can only judge a tree by its fruit. He tells us that a good tree can only bear good fruit, and a bad tree can only bear bad fruit, despite what may appear on the surface to be to the contrary. The proof is in the fruit, not in the appearances (Matthew 7:16-23). If the Spirit of God is motivating us, we will bring forth His fruits in our lives; if the spirit of the world, or of the flesh, or of the devil is motivating us, we will produce quite different fruits in our lives.

We can only judge the Holy Spirit's presence and working in us if we ask ourselves honestly: are we growing in love, joy, peace, patient endurance, generosity, faith, mildness, chastity, continence, and modesty (Galatians 5:22-23)? Just as the wind can only be known by its effects, so, too, the Holy Spirit can only be genuinely known by the effects of His fruits in our spiritual lives.

Wind and Breath: Symbols of the Spirit of Life

Gentle as a Breeze, Powerful as a Hurricane

As for the force of the wind, that varies quite a bit. Sometimes it is a gentle breeze which can be very refreshing on a warm summer day. Sometimes the wind can be fierce and powerful as in a gale or hurricane. Sometimes the wind can speed us up when it is to our backs or hinder us if we are moving against it.[2]

Like the wind, the force of the Spirit varies in our lives. Most often the Spirit's lead is gentle, almost imperceptible. He inspires us in a low-key way, and nudges us along, slowly but surely. (After all, there are many more gentle breezes in life than there are hurricanes!) But there are also times when the Spirit is unmistakably directing us in a certain way. We get the message "loud and clear"; there is no mistaking what He wants of us. These are the times when the Spirit's promptings are forceful and undeniable. We may even want to avoid them or run from them. Do we not often resist, for example, His inspirations to greater generosity in service and sacrifice? How many people try to run from the thought of serving God in the Priesthood or Religious life? Like Jeremiah, we invent all kinds of excuses to God's call:

Ah, Lord God! I know not how to speak; I am too young! (Jeremiah 1:6)

If the Holy Spirit wants us, there is ultimately no way to escape His prompting, nowhere to run from Him. It is like a situation involving a secondhand car that someone once donated to our Renewal Community in the South Bronx. It had two big dents in the roof. I was told that they were caused by a hurricane. Prior to the storm the owner had moved the car to a "safe place." As it happened, the only tree in the whole area that was knocked over by the wind fell and hit this particular car. There are times when there is absolutely no "safe place" to run to and hide from the Spirit!

81

BREATH

The second life symbol that relates to the Holy Spirit is breath. For ancient peoples, breath, like wind, had a mysterious quality. For the Hebrews, a person's breath was the source of life. The account of the creation of Adam is an example of this:

> The Lord God formed man out of the clay of the ground and blew into his nostrils the breath of life, and so man became a living being. (Genesis 2:7)

The Breath of Life for All Creation

Human breath was seen as the breath of God in us. His breath was thought to give life to us as well as to all creation; furthermore, it kept all things in existence. The Psalmist expresses this thought about all God's creatures in a striking way:

> All (living creatures) look to You to give them food in due time. When You give it to them, they gather it; when You open Your hand, they are filled with good things. If you hide Your face, they are dismayed; if You take away their breath, they perish and return to their dust. When You send forth Your spirit, they are created and You renew the face of the earth. (Psalm 104:27-30)

The Breath of Our Spiritual Life

In our spiritual life, it is the Holy Spirit, as the Breath of God, Who breathes into us the spark of divine life. His presence in the soul is the origin of our supernatural life. His continued guidance is the means of sustaining the divine life of Sanctifying Grace in us and allowing us to continue to grow. This is the literal meaning of the word "inspiration"; it comes from the Latin "in spirare" — "to breathe into." The Holy Spirit is then the breath of God blowing in us. One of the hymns suggested for use in the "Liturgy of the Hours" captures this sentiment:

Wind and Breath: Symbols of the Spirit of Life

Breathe on me, Breath of God,
fill me with life anew,
That I may love the things You love,
and do what You would do.

Breathe on me, Breath of God,
until my heart is pure,
Until with You I have one will,
to live and to endure.

Breathe on me, Breath of God,
my soul with grace refine,
Until this earthly part of me,
glows with Your fire divine.

Breathe on me, Breath of God,
so I shall never die,
But live with You the perfect life
in Your eternity.

(Music by H.E. Wooldridge, 1845-1917; Text by Edwin Hatch, 1835-1889; and adapted by Anthony G. Petti, as quoted in *The Liturgy of the Hours*, Vol. 4, Catholic Book Publishing Co., New York, 1975, p. 623-624.)

As we have already seen, this new life of the Holy Spirit was given to us at the time of our Baptism. Jesus referred to Baptism as a new life "from above." Now just as the natural life of our body must grow, so, too, the new supernatural life in our soul must grow. In our natural human life, the process of growth and development flows from an internal source of life (our soul), and it matures according to laws and norms God has preordained for human growth. In our supernatural life the internal source of life is the Holy Spirit Himself. Dwelling within our souls, He guides the unfolding and maturing of the life of grace according to the laws He has preordained; at the same time, He still maintains His freedom to move in us as He wills. He leads no two people exactly alike. We all receive different gifts of nature and grace. We all are entrusted with different works and ministries from the Lord.

Our "second wind"

St. Augustine tells us that once we have begun the journey of our spiritual life the road becomes long and monotonous. Our Lord Himself tells us that the Divine Bridegroom delays His coming (Matthew 25:5). Our lifetime here on earth is a period of continuous effort to live faithful Catholic Christian lives. At times, it can appear like a seemingly endless waiting for the Lord's return. This takes its toll on many. Some grow weary and barely manage to trudge along; others lose their way for awhile; still others abandon the struggle altogether. It is at this point of weariness or discouragement that the Spirit of Life sustains and renews us throughout our long journey. Like a runner in a marathon race, we need a new breath of fresh air, our "second wind," in order to have the energy to endure to the end. The Holy Spirit breathes that spiritual "second wind" into our lives just when we need it.

Renewal within

Today there is a lot of talk about people who experience such countless demands and constant pressures in their lives that they end up with the symptom known as "burn out." These people have given so much that there seems to be nothing left to give. They feel spent physically, emotionally, mentally, and spiritually. They are exhausted with life. The opposite of those suffering from "burn out" are those suffering from "rust out." They, too, are exhausted and bored with life, simply because they have not given of themselves in any way. Both groups of people need to be renewed.

Jesus invites us to come to Him in just such circumstances:

Come to Me, all you who are weary and find life burdensome, and I will refresh you. Take My yoke upon your shoulders and learn from Me, for I am gentle and humble of heart. Your souls will find rest, for My yoke is easy and My burden light. (Matthew 11:28-30)

And how does Jesus refresh us? Precisely by sending us His Holy Spirit Who constantly revives and renews us along the journey of life. The Fathers of the Church used to love to compare the Holy Spirit to a precious ointment whose fragrance constantly renews the vessel that contains it. We are those vessels! In our spiritual lives — when we begin to lose our fervor and are in danger of falling into a state or an attitude of mediocrity, lukewarmness and indifference — the Holy Spirit breathes back into us renewed life. We pray for this renewal in the sentiments of the "Golden Sequence" from the Mass of Pentecost:

> Bend the stubborn heart and will,
> Melt the frozen, warm the chill;
> Guide the steps that go astray.
>
> Heal our wounds, our strength renew;
> On our dryness, pour Thy dew;
> Wash the stains of guilt away.

The Spirit Keeps Us from Despair

Sometimes we may even feel we have reached the point of despair. We may believe that we are at the end of our rope and we just do not seem to be able to hang on any longer. This can happen in experiences which St. John of the Cross called the "dark night." God may seem very far away, quite unconcerned. Like the frightening experience the Apostles once had on the Sea of Galilee, we may well feel that the Lord is apparently fast asleep while we are battling the storms of life that appear to be overwhelming us:

It happened that a bad squall blew up. The waves were breaking over the boat and it began to ship water badly. Jesus was in the stern through it all, sound asleep on a cushion. They finally woke Him and said to Him: "Teacher, does it not matter to You that we are going to drown?" (Mark 4:37-38)

Our human situation may seem to be without any possible solution. All seems lost! If our spiritual lives are genuine, we will inevitably experience such circumstances. All apparent reason to hope or to continue on the journey will seem gone! This is precisely when the Spirit of Life comes to renew us.

The Prophet Ezekiel's Message of Hope through the Spirit

One of those in Scripture who experienced this so strikingly was the prophet Ezekiel. He was called to be a prophet during the exile of the Jewish people in Babylon. If there was a time in their history when things were bleak, it was in Babylon. We catch a glimpse of this in the powerful sentiments of the Psalmist:

> By the streams of Babylon we sat and wept when we remembered Zion. On the aspens of that land we hung up our harps though there our captors asked of us the lyrics of our songs, and our despoilers urged us to be joyous, "Sing for us the songs of Zion!" How could we sing a song of the Lord in a foreign land? If I forget you, Jerusalem, may my right hand be forgotten! May my tongue cleave to my palate if I remember you not, if I place not Jerusalem ahead of my joy! (Psalm 137:1-6)

The Jewish exiles feel a sense of despair

There was reason to feel as they did. Prior to the exile, the people had been unfaithful to God and to their covenant with Him. They had offended God by their sins of idolatry, immorality, and apostasy. Divine punishment came with the fall of Jerusalem, the destruction of the Temple, and the exile of the people into slavery by the Babylonians. They were in exile for approximately fifty years. They were beginning to feel abandoned by God forever! Did He love His people any longer?

Deutero-Isaiah, another prophet of this painful era, reflected their cry of despair. At the same time, He also reminded them of God's enduring love for them throughout this period of their trial in exile:

Sing out, O heavens, and rejoice, O earth, break forth into song, you mountains. For the Lord comforts His people and shows mercy to His afflicted. But Zion said: "The Lord has forsaken me; my Lord has forgotten me." Can a mother forget her infant, be without tenderness for the child of her womb? Even should she forget, I will never forget you. See, upon the palms of My hands I have written your name. (Isaiah 49:13-16)

God's promises of a restoration

The Lord would deliver His people. Ezekiel was to be the chief prophet of this message of hope. He proclaimed a restoration that would involve "clean water," a "new heart," and a "new spirit."

The Lord God said: "I will take you away from among the nations, gather you from all the foreign lands, and bring you back to your own land. I will sprinkle clean water upon you to cleanse you from all your impurities, and from all your idols I will cleanse you. I will give you a new heart and place a new spirit within you, taking from your bodies your stony hearts and giving you natural hearts. I will put My spirit within you and make you live by My statutes, careful to observe My decrees. You shall live in the land I gave your fathers; you shall be My people, and I will be your God." (Ezekiel 36:24-28)

For a Jewish person in exile in Babylon, far away from his native Israel, this was indeed a comforting message. With the "clean water," God would wash away the filth of the sins of His people. With a "new heart," God would give His people a new attitude and outlook to replace the hardness of heart they had shown in resisting His call of love. With a "new spirit," God would breathe into His people a new life and give them a moral strength that would enable them to observe faithfully His commandments.[3]

The Spirit as the breath of God renews His people

One final and very important part of Ezekiel's message of hope and restoration links the breath of the Spirit with the renewing of the life of God's people. It is described in the prophet's famous vision of the dry bones.[4] In this vision Ezekiel found himself in the middle of a broad plain filled with lifeless bones:

How dry they were! (Ezekiel 37:2)

These dry bones represented the people in their brokenness, helplessness, and hopelessness! The Lord then commanded Ezekiel to prophesy over the dry bones so that they would come together in unity again, and so that sinews, flesh, and skin would grow and cover them.

I prophesied as I had been told, and even as I was prophesying I heard a noise; it was a rattling as the bones came together, bone joining bone. I saw the sinews and the flesh come upon them, and the skin cover them, but there was no spirit in them. (Ezekiel 37:7-8)

Then the Lord commanded him to prophesy that "spirit" would come into the bones now covered with flesh, so that they might come to life again. Ezekiel shared his experience as follows:

Then He said to me: "Prophesy to the spirit, prophesy, son of man, and say to the spirit, Thus says the Lord God: From the four winds come O spirit, and breathe into these slain that they may come to life." I prophesied as He told me, and the spirit came into them; they came alive and stood upright, a vast army. Then He said to me: "Son of man, these bones are the whole house of Israel. They have been saying, 'Our bones are dried up, our hope is lost, and we are cut off.' Therefore, prophesy and say to them: Thus says the Lord God: O My people, I will open your graves and have you rise from them, and bring you back to the land of Israel. Then you shall know that I am the Lord, when I open your graves and have you rise from them, O My people! I will put My spirit in you that you may live, and I will settle you upon your land; thus you shall know that I am the Lord. I have promised, and I will do it, says the Lord." (Ezekiel 37:9-14)

Just as it was not until "spirit" entered into the dry bones covered with sinews and flesh that they finally revived, so without the Spirit of Life in us we cannot be continuously revived and renewed in our spiritual lives. We would be in danger of languishing under the burdens and pressures of each day. It might even reach the point where it seems that any hope or trust within us is dying. We are ready to abandon the struggle. "Why continue?" we ask ourselves. But in reality, all is not lost; we have not yet "given up the ghost" so to speak. Someone once put up a humorous sign in a friary where I was stationed some years ago: "For those of you who don't believe the dead can come back to life, you ought to be here at quitting time." If it can happen in our natural lives that we can "come back to life," how much more so will it happen in our Christian lives!

When an emergency rescue team worker goes to the aid of various people, he or she often has to administer mouth-to-mouth resuscitation techniques. The breath of the person who is healthy can supply and restore the breath of the person in need. When this occurs in our spiritual lives, it is a sign that the Spirit of Life as the breath of God is reviving our drooping spirits and restoring us, once again, to a fuller share in Christ's life.

Footnotes

1. *The Merriam-Webster Dictionary*, Pocket Books, New York, 1974, p. 693.
2. I remember a round trip between the United States and Europe that I was on some years ago. On the way to Europe the jumbo jet experienced a strong tailwind and cruised at about 580 miles per hour; one week later, on the return flight, there was a headwind of 70 to 100 miles per hour and the same jumbo jet averaged only about 460 miles per hour. Needless to say, it was a much longer flight back to the United States!
3. From our New Testament viewpoint we can see an even "fuller sense" in this Old Testament prophecy. It refers to the "new covenant" established by Our Lord through His death and Resurrection — the new "cleansing water" and the "new spirit" refer to the Sacrament of Baptism which would be a new birth by water and the Holy Spirit as Our Lord later told Nicodemus.
4. This is the vision that was made popular by the old spiritual hymn, "Them Bones, Them Bones!"

Chapter 8

Additional Symbols of
the Spirit of Life: Water and Fire

THE SYMBOLS DEALT WITH in the previous chapter, wind and breath, are of a more mysterious quality than the symbols of water and fire that we will focus on in this chapter. These latter symbols are more obvious to our senses. They are also rich in imagery that can help us better understand the Spirit of Life and His role in our Christian lives.

WATER

A third life-symbol that relates to the Holy Spirit is water. Water's natural symbolism lends itself easily to themes of life, since all living creatures depend on water to some degree for survival.

Old Testament Symbolism of Water

Therefore, it is not surprising that throughout the Scriptures water has a rich life-symbolism. This is reflected in the fact that the Church, particularly during the blessing of the water to be used at her Baptismal liturgy, makes reference to several Old Testament passages where water symbolizes life and salvation. For example, the flood waters in the story of Noah are used as a sign of the destruction of sin and the preservation of those who are just. In the story of the Israelites' crossing of the Red Sea, the parting of the waters is a symbol of the waters of Baptism. By passing through those waters the Israelites became free while their enemies, the Egyptians, were destroyed. In Baptism, we are likewise set free to become children of God through the new life of the Trinity we possess. Through the waters of Baptism we are freed of Original Sin and, in the case of adults, also of personal sins. Further, the abundant water that flowed from the rock Moses struck in the desert to give drink to the Israelite people is also a symbol of the Holy Spirit.[1] It represents the Living Water that flows into our souls through Baptism, and refreshes us to continue our journey through life.

Examples in the Gospel of St. John

In the New Testament the symbol of water frequently refers to the Spirit as Life-Giver. This is especially true in the Gospel of St. John. His Gospel is filled with symbolism that refers to the various sacraments Christ instituted as means of grace, particularly Baptism and the Holy Eucharist.

Jesus meets the Samaritan woman at the well

One such reference is found in Our Lord's conversation with the Samaritan woman at the well (John 4:4-42). As we have already looked at this incident, let us now simply review it very briefly. Our Lord, tired and thirsty from a long journey, stops at a well in the rather hostile territory of Samaria. He asks for a drink from a woman who has come to draw water. Indignant that He, a Jewish man, would publicly speak to her, a Samaritan woman, she opposes Him at first. However, His kindness eventually wins her confidence. He then goes on to reveal to her all He can give her.

> If only you recognized God's Gift, and Who it is that is asking you for a drink, you would have asked Him instead, and He would have given you living water. (John 4:10)

Additional Symbols of the Spirit of Life: Water and Fire

The Spirit as "Living Water"

Actually we have two references in this passage to the Holy Spirit. The first reference is to the Holy Spirit as the "Gift of God," which we have already examined in some depth. But the second reference is to the Holy Spirit as "Living Water." He will be poured forth into our souls to give us spiritual life, much as water poured on plants sustains them and when needed, even revives them. In his Gospel, St. John refers to water as a symbol of the life-giving Spirit. Jesus explains to the Samaritan woman the effect of this Living Water.

> Everyone who drinks this water (in the well) will be thirsty again. But whoever drinks the water I give him will never be thirsty; no, the water I give shall become a fountain within him, leaping up to provide eternal life. (John 4:13-14)

Our Lord here contrasts the "stagnant water" in the well, which can only satisfy our natural bodily thirst for a little while, with the "Living Water" He wants to give us, the Holy Spirit Who would satisfy the thirst of our soul. Jesus goes on to say that when we receive this Living Water, it becomes like a fountain within us, springing up to provide eternal life. This is precisely the Spirit's role — to be the constant source of Eternal Life within our souls!

Jesus solemnly promises the Spirit at the Feast of Booths

In another incident of his Gospel, St. John again refers to water as a symbol of the life-giving Spirit. It takes place on the last day of the great Jewish Festival of Booths, sometimes called the "Feast of Tabernacles" or, in Hebrew, the "Feast of Succoth." It was the most joyful of the Jewish feasts. It occurred at the time of the grape harvest which coincided with the end of the wheat harvest. It was also the time for the Jewish people to pray to God to send abundant rain upon their fields. This was necessary to insure that the crops in the following year would be plentiful.

During this festival there was a very solemn ceremony involving water. Each morning of the week-long festival, a group of priests and people walked in procession through the gate in the city wall known as the "Watergate." They proceeded down to the fountain of Gihon on the side of the hill of the Temple. This fountain supplied the water for the pool of Siloam.[2] One of the priests then filled a golden pitcher with water from the fountain. While this was done, the choir chanted a verse from the prophet Isaiah: "With joy you will draw water at the fountain of salvation" (Isaiah 12:3). Then, singing various psalms, they returned in procession to the Temple. When the procession reached the altar of holocausts, the people in procession marched around the altar and sang: "O Lord, grant salvation! O Lord, grant prosperity!" (Psalm 118:25).

On each of the first six days of the festival, the procession marched only once around the altar; on the last and greatest day of the festival, the procession marched seven times around the altar. Then the priest approached the ramp to the altar to pour the water into a silver funnel from where it flowed out onto the ground. This was a sign of their awaiting the abundant rains God would send upon their fields. It was at this dramatic moment in the festival ceremony that St. John tells us:

> On the last and greatest day of the festival, Jesus stood up and cried out: "If anyone thirsts, let him come to Me; let him drink who believes in Me. Scripture has it: From within Him rivers of living water shall flow." (John 7:37-38)

The Spirit as a fountain within us

This "Living Water" becomes as a spring or fountain within the soul of everyone who comes to believe in Jesus. St. John observes:

> Here Jesus was referring to the Spirit, Whom those that came to believe in Him were to receive. There was, of course, no Spirit as yet, since Jesus had not yet been glorified. (John 7:39)

What Our Blessed Lord promised then is that those who come

to Him thirsting for the Living Water of the Spirit will receive it in abundance. The Spirit will flow as living water from the Heart of Christ into the heart of the individual, and there the Spirit will become like a Fountain. Just as a spring of water in a desert land can produce a life of rich vegetation, so, too, the Spirit in us will bring our soul to life and will allow us to bring forth the fruits of Christian holiness. This is reflected in Psalm 1 where we find a description of a faithful God-loving person who is really deeply rooted in the Holy Spirit. Such a person is described as being:

> Like a tree planted near running water, that yields its fruit in due season, and whose leaves never fade. Whatever he does, prospers. (Psalm 1:3)

Thus, a good person — one deeply rooted in the Holy Spirit — is like "a tree planted near running water." Even in a desert, the roots of a tree planted near flowing water can sink down to a hidden underground spring that feeds the river or stream or more often reaches to the bed of the stream itself to get its needed water. In any event, the tree will always have a vital water supply. This accounts for the effects produced. Its leaves never fade but retain their vital texture all year round. Furthermore, such a tree "yields its fruit in due season." Being alive and thriving, despite the hot sun, the tree will produce its own fruit once or twice during the year at its appointed season(s).

All this beautiful imagery describes the soul of someone rooted in the "Living Water," the Holy Spirit. It will never be in danger of withering for lack of moisture because the Spirit will be a constant fountain of spiritual refreshment, vitality, and strength within it. The Spirit's working in us will produce an abundant harvest of the appropriate virtues of the Christian life. This Fountain of Living Water will bring forth various fruits in our daily lives if only we remain firmly rooted in grace and generously follow the inspirations we receive. The Second Vatican Council teaches this clearly in its most important document, *The Dogmatic Constitution on the Church*:

The Holy Spirit was sent on the day of Pentecost in order that He might continually sanctify the Church, and that, consequently, those who believe might have access through Christ in one Spirit to the Father. He is the Spirit of Life, the fountain of water springing up to eternal life. To men, dead in sin, the Father gives life through Him, until the day when, in Christ, He raises to life their mortal bodies. The Spirit dwells in the Church and in the hearts of the faithful, as in a temple... He bestows upon (the Church) various hierarchic and charismatic gifts, and in this way directs her; and He adorns her with His fruits. By the power of the Gospel He permits the Church to keep the freshness of youth. Constantly He renews her and leads her to perfect union with her Spouse (Jesus). (*Lumen Gentium*, par. 4)

Symbol of Thirst and Cleansing

We can draw one further comparison between water as a life symbol and the Holy Spirit when we look at the very nature of water itself and its usefulness. Two of its most basic uses are for drinking and for bathing. We must drink water because we need it to sustain our bodily functions. Perhaps we get an idea why Jesus said that if anyone gives a cup of cold water in His Name they would not lose their reward (Matthew 10:24). In a similar way, the Spirit gives us supernatural life as the Living Water of our souls. A second natural use of water is for bathing. In this symbolism we find reflected the sense of the Spirit cleansing us of our sins, thereby freeing us from the guilt we have incurred because of them.

Thirsting for the Spirit

On our part there must be a corresponding desire or thirst for the Living Water of the Holy Spirit in our hearts. We can actually distinguish two kinds of thirst, each caused by a different factor. One kind is caused by deprivation. An example of this is the thirst people suffer during a time of drought. This is quite a "negative" thirst because it is due to a lack of something essential. Drought often brings a scorching of the earth and leads to a lack of crops and then of food in general, thereby threatening people with death by starvation. Similarly, a drought of the Spirit means we do not possess Him Who is the Source of all life within us. Our life in Christ is then in danger of dying for lack of the "Living Water" that we all need. Such a thirst would be totally negative and undesirable.

On the other hand, there is a thirst or desire that is quite "positive" because it is created by a definite longing. On a very hot day, a person can long to drink his or her favorite cold beverage such as iced tea, soda, beer, or lemonade. This is delightful and refreshing. Likewise, our thirst for the Spirit makes us seek Him more ardently and constantly. When we drink of the "Living Water," our soul experiences joy and refreshment. In this thirst, the soul yearns for God as the satisfaction of all its desires. This thirst or longing is very positive and quite desirable. This is often used as an image of prayer in the Scriptures, especially in the Psalms:

> As the hind longs for the running waters, so my soul longs for You, O God. Athirst is my soul for God, the living God. When shall I go and behold the face of God? (Psalm 42:2-4)
> O God, You are my God Whom I seek; for You my flesh pines and my soul thirsts like the earth, parched, lifeless and without water. Thus have I gazed toward You in the sanctuary to see Your power and your glory. For Your kindness is a greater good than life; my lips shall glorify You. (Psalm 63:2-4)

This thirst for the Living Water of the Holy Spirit is no doubt part of that thirst Jesus blessed when He called those blessed who hungered and thirsted for holiness! He said they would be satisfied (Matthew 5:6).

FIRE

A fourth and final symbol relating to the Spirit of Life is fire. Like water, it is a very rich symbol.

Fire Is Linked to the Spirit in Scripture

In the Old Testament, fire was often a mysterious sign of God's presence. For example, God first spoke to Moses from a bush that was burning but not consumed by the fire (Exodus 3:2). When God went ahead of His people to lead them on their journey through the desert, His presence was signified by a column of cloud by day and a column of fire by night (Exodus 13:21). In the great "theophany" or manifestation by God of Himself to Moses and all the people at Mt. Sinai we read that the mountain was:

> all wrapped in smoke, for the Lord came down upon it in fire. (Exodus 19:18)

In the New Testament, St. John the Baptist links fire in a special way to the Holy Spirit. In contrasting the baptism he administered with the Baptism Jesus would give, he says:

> I baptize you in water for the sake of reform, but the One Who will follow me is more powerful than I. I am not even fit to carry His sandals. He it is Who will baptize you in the Holy Spirit and fire. (Luke 3:16)

Our Lord Himself later said of His purpose in coming among us:

> I have come to light a fire on the earth. How I wish the blaze were ignited. (Luke 12:49)

We have received that fire in the Holy Spirit. When He came on Pentecost there was a kind of fire as the sign of His presence:

> Tongues as of fire appeared, which parted and came to rest on each of them. All were filled with the Holy Spirit. They began to express themselves in foreign tongues and make bold proclamation as the Spirit prompted them. (Acts 2:3-4)

The Effects of the Fire of the Spirit in Us

Fire: a natural symbol

We can learn something about the Holy Spirit's working in us from the very nature of fire. Fire gives us light and warmth; the Holy Spirit gives us these in a spiritual sense. By His light, the Holy Spirit assists our minds to know the Lord and the truths He has revealed to us. By His warmth, the Holy Spirit moves our wills. This enables us to follow with eagerness and determination a course of action which will work to God's greater glory, to our salvation and sanctification, and to the building up of the Church, the Mystical Body of Christ.

Fire also has the capability of purifying, as when steel is placed in intense fire and all foreign elements are burned away. The Holy Spirit's fire cleanses us of our sins and sinful attachments, freeing our hearts so that we may belong entirely to the Lord.

Fire: a mystical symbol

In addition to its natural symbolism, fire also relates to life with a somewhat mystical meaning. When a person seems very happy or excited about something or anxious to do something, we sometimes say "they are all fired up." We have already seen how the ancient Greeks viewed this "fire" as a spark of divine life in a person. That is why they coined the word "enthusiasm" which means literally "in God" or "God within the person."

I remember an example of such enthusiasm from the years when I taught Religion in Catholic high school. Before all the big football games there was always a lot of excitement in the school among both the faculty and the students. Many times the students decorated bulletin boards in preparation for the game. Signs adorned the hallways. Inevitably there was the message: "Catch the spirit!" And the high point of preparation for the homecoming football game was the rally the night before when everyone stood around the traditional bonfire. All this was to "fire up the spirit to win."

The Fire of Zeal Is Stirred Up Within Us

The symbolism of this aspect of fire relates to the virtue of zeal for the cause of Christ. Christian zeal is the enthusiasm and determination to do all we can to spread the Good News of Jesus. It is motivated by love. It can express itself in many different ways for the building up of the Kingdom of God.

The "tongues as of fire" which appeared over the heads of the disciples on Pentecost signified not only their reception of the Holy Spirit, but also prefigured the zeal that would characterize their preaching of the Gospel message. In fact, they immediately began to make "bold proclamation as the Spirit prompted them" (Acts 2:4). The disciples had been fearful up to this time. Now they were bold, because their zeal enabled them to set their doubts aside and overcome their fears. This same zeal characterized the Apostles in the carrying out of their mission to spread the Kingdom of God. Similarly, this ardent zeal characterized the saints of all ages in the Church's history. It enabled them to make great sacrifices, persevere in the face of difficult struggles, and overcome almost insurmountable opposition to spread the Kingdom of Christ. As Our Lord said:

> From John the Baptizer's time until now the Kingdom of God has suffered violence, and the violent take it by force. (Matthew 11:12)

"Violence" is used here by Our Lord not in any negative or morally bad sense of doing harm to others, but in a positive sense of determination to do good, no matter what it costs. The violent, then, are those who are moved by zeal for the sake of Christ and of His Kingdom. The zealous Apostle, St. Paul, wrote to his young assistant, Timothy, of the need to continually renew the apostolic zeal he received through the Gift of the Holy Spirit:

> I remind you to stir into flame the Gift of God bestowed when my hands were laid on you. The Spirit God has given us is no cowardly spirit, but rather one that makes us strong, loving and wise. (2 Timothy 1:6-7)

Additional Symbols of the Spirit of Life: Water and Fire

It is in this same sense that we pray in the traditional prayer to the Holy Spirit: "Come, Holy Spirit, fill the hearts of Your faithful, and enkindle in them the fire of Your Divine Love."

A final story might illustrate this point. Vince Lombardi, the great football coach, was once asked by a reporter, "What is the secret of a great coach?" Lombardi answered:

> The great coaches are not those who can draw diagrams of plays on a chalkboard; these coaches are a dime a dozen. But the really great coach is the one who can get his own spirit to win and communicate it to his players so that when they go out on that playing field they are playing with his spirit to win!

When I read that story I thought to myself, "Isn't that what Our Lord has done for us? Hasn't He given us His Spirit so that when we go forth we will be moved by the same Spirit that was within Him?" What a blessing Jesus has given us, that He shares the fire of the Holy Spirit with us!

Footnotes

1. St. Paul saw the "rock" as a reference to Jesus, Who gives us the Living Water, the Holy Spirit (cf. 1 Corinthians 10:4).
2. This was the same pool to which Our Lord in St. John's Gospel had sent the blind man to wash his eyes and after washing, the blind man received his sight (John 9).

III.

THE HOLY SPIRIT: THE SPIRIT OF COURAGE

Chapter 9

The Holy Spirit Strengthens Us in the Struggles of Life

ALL FOUR OF THE GOSPEL WRITERS begin their accounts of Our Lord's public ministry with His baptism in the Jordan River by St. John the Baptist. Each presents the baptism as a "theophany" or visible manifestation of the Blessed Trinity: God the Father speaks; Jesus is proclaimed as the Father's beloved Son; the Holy Spirit is revealed in the form of a dove. St. Luke, for example, describes Jesus' baptism this way:

> When all the people were baptized and Jesus was at prayer after likewise being baptized, the skies opened and the Holy Spirit descended on Him in visible form like a dove. A voice from Heaven was heard to say, "You are My beloved Son. On You My favor rests." (Luke 3:21-22)

WHY WAS JESUS BAPTIZED?

It is important for us to understand why Jesus was baptized. There were a number of reasons.

To Identify With Our Sinfulness

One reason was so that Our Lord could identify with our sinfulness. We must bear in mind that people who accepted the baptism which St. John preached were acknowledging their sins and awaiting the promised Messiah.

Jesus Himself was absolutely sinless. He personally had no need to be baptized. As the Fathers of the Church liked to point out, the waters of the Jordan could not sanctify Jesus, but He could sanctify the waters of the Jordan! By undergoing the baptism St. John was administering for "sinners" to repent, Jesus was identifying Himself with our sinfulness.

Interestingly, even the Baptist at first hesitated when Our Lord approached him to be baptized (Matthew 3:13-15). St. John recognized His surpassing holiness and acknowledged his own unworthiness to baptize Him.

To Prefigure the Sacrament of Baptism

A second reason Jesus was baptized was that by His own baptism He was prefiguring the Sacrament of Baptism He would later institute for His Church. Unlike the baptism of water that John administered, Jesus would give us a Baptism of water and the Holy Spirit. By our own Christian Baptism, we would come to share in the redemption Jesus won for us by His saving Death!

Anointed With the Spirit to Begin His Mission

Finally, Jesus was baptized in order to experience a visible "anointing" with the Holy Spirit to prepare Him for His mission as the Messiah. "Messiah" is a Hebrew word that means "The Anointed One." The Greek word for "Anointed One" is the title "Christos" (Christ). The Jewish people in the Old Testament were accustomed to anoint their kings, their prophets, and their priests. Accordingly, they gave the title "Messiah" to the One whom they were awaiting, the One whom God had promised to send to them. They used this title because the One to come would be greater than any of their kings, or prophets, or priests! He would truly be "The Anointed One"!

The prophet Isaiah had said of the Suffering Servant, the promised Messiah, that He would be anointed with the Spirit.

> Here is My Servant whom I uphold, My Chosen One with whom I am pleased, upon whom I have put My spirit; He shall bring forth justice to the nations. (Isaiah 42:1)[1]

The Holy Spirit's descent upon Jesus at His baptism was the precise sign by which St. John himself would know that Jesus was the One Whom the Father had sent. In fact, he testified to this:

> John gave this testimony also: "I saw the Spirit descend like a dove from the sky, and it came to rest on Him. But I did not recognize Him. The One Who sent me to baptize with water told me: 'When you see the Spirit descend and rest on someone, it is He Who is to baptize with the Holy Spirit.' Now I have seen for myself and have testified: 'This is God's Chosen One.'" (John 1:32-34)

This witness of St. John the Baptist is important because it tells us not only that the Spirit came upon Jesus but that the Spirit "rested" upon Him; the Spirit remained with Jesus. In this way, Jesus possessed a fullness of the Holy Spirit. From this fullness, then, Jesus, as Messiah, could give the Spirit to others.[2]

"SPIRITUAL WARFARE"

Once Jesus had been baptized in the Jordan, His public ministry was ready to begin. Now what is the very first thing that happens? St. Luke describes it for us:

> Jesus, full of the Holy Spirit, then returned from the Jordan and was conducted by the Spirit into the desert for forty days, where He was tempted by the devil. (Luke 4:1-2)

As soon as Our Lord is ready to begin His public ministry, the first thing He encounters is trial and temptation. St. Luke's words emphasize the fact that the Holy Spirit "drove" Jesus into the desert!

There is a sense of compulsion, a driving force as if Jesus had to go out of some necessity.

And where does the Holy Spirit lead Our Lord? Into the desert! Why? Physically, the desert was a wilderness; it was a barren, rugged, stark reality inhabited only by a few wild animals. There was nothing there to distract a person! As a result, the desert was a place where a person could not hide from confrontation.

This confrontation could take many possible forms. Maybe it could be a confrontation with God. With no place to hide, the desert could easily bring a person face-to-face with God. For many people, this would not be very pleasant. The individual might end up "wrestling" with God in honest heart-to-heart prayer, like Jacob wrestling with God's messenger in the wilderness (cf. Genesis 32:23-33). Jesus would one day literally agonize over the Will of His Heavenly Father in the Garden of Gethsemane, but there was no confrontation with His Heavenly Father in prayer in the desert.

At other times there is a confrontation with one's self in the desert. With no distractions to divert one's attention, a person in the desert might be faced with his or her most hidden thoughts or perhaps some deep, secret recesses of the heart. Many who went out to the desert hoping, like Moses, to see a "burning bush," found only "shades of darkness" within themselves instead! Because Jesus did not have a "shadow side," He did not have this kind of confrontation with Himself in the desert.

Finally, there is the possibility of a confrontation with evil spirits. In biblical times the desert was especially thought of as the dwelling place of demons. The devils, with all their cunning temptations, might try to lead the unsuspecting and the careless to a fall into sin. This was Our Lord's confrontation in the desert — with Satan himself. He had led our first parents into the Original Sin and their descendants into so many personal sins thereafter.

St. Mark describes Jesus' experience after His baptism:

> At that point the Spirit sent Him out toward the desert. He stayed in the wasteland forty days, put to the test there by Satan. (Mark 1:12-13)

Thus, the desert was a veritable battleground, the setting for "spiritual warfare." The Israelites, after passing through the waters of the Red Sea, were led by God on a journey into the desert; the desert proved to be a place of testing and trials for them. So, too, Jesus after His baptism was driven by the Holy Spirit into the desert that He might begin, through testing and temptations, to fight the devil on his own "territory."

We Confront the Powers of Evil in Our Own Lives

Anyone who begins to live the spiritual life in earnest likewise experiences a "spiritual warfare." St. Paul and St. Barnabas encouraged the converts they made on their very first missionary journey with the instruction:

> We must undergo many trials if we are to enter into the reign of God. (Acts 14:22)

Whenever we receive the power of the Holy Spirit we will inevitably come into conflict with the cunning deceit of the Evil Spirit as well as with the "shadows" of our own human spirit. This is why it is said that there are three "spirits" involved in our spiritual struggle. First, there is the human spirit, our soul; this is the place where the spiritual conflict, in a sense, is being waged. Second, there is the Evil Spirit, who tries by his temptations and his deceit to lead us away from God. Third, there is the Holy Spirit Who possesses our souls by His indwelling. By His inspirations, He defends us from evil and moves us to do good.

Each person, then, who begins living the Christian life and seriously grows in that life, will inevitably come to trials. It is like riding a bicycle. If you ride it downhill, it is enjoyable. There is almost no effort to peddle the bike. Gravity is in the rider's favor. However, once you try to ride that same bicycle uphill, you immediately experience gravity's adverse effects. The rider realizes there is a force pulling in the opposite direction.

We experience something similar in the spiritual life. If we were leading sinful and selfish lives, it would all seem easy, because we would be going spiritually *downhill*! Going along with one's passions and sinful inclinations is easy. We are gratifying what gives us pleasure. If, however, we tried to do good, we would encounter resistance, because we would then be moving morally *uphill*! We would find that the self-denial required to control our sinful passions goes against the grain, while the energy and determination needed to practice virtue costs a great deal of effort.

"Soldiers of Christ"

The early Christians were very conscious that the spiritual life was often a kind of spiritual warfare. In fact, in the early centuries of the Church, Christian men and women by the thousands, some as solitary hermits and others in early religious communities, took to the deserts of Egypt, Syria, and Palestine in search of greater holiness through lives of prayer and detachment. They knew that, like Jesus, they would confront the devils in these deserts with their cunning and frightening temptations. But they went out fearlessly as "soldiers of Christ," (in Latin, "miles Christi"), "warriors of God," to do battle against their spiritual enemies.

Their battle was also partly against themselves, for it included struggling against and subduing their own passions and disordered inclinations. They understood well the teaching of St. Paul that the only way to obtain the "fruits of the Spirit" was to eradicate the "fruits of the flesh" from their lives. This would involve a long and often bitter struggle, a veritable crucifixion of self-centeredness. It would be a fight to the finish between a true and proper self-love that leads to love of God and love of neighbor, and a false self-love that leads only to love of our own ego! St. Paul put it in unmistakably clear language:

> My point is that you should live in accord with the Spirit and you will not yield to the cravings of the flesh. The flesh lusts against the Spirit and the Spirit against the flesh; the two are directly opposed... Those who belong to Christ Jesus have

crucified their flesh with its passions and desires. Since we live by the Spirit, let us follow the Spirit's lead. (Galatians 5:16-17, 24-25)

These early Christians knew that if they persevered in the struggle, they would, by God's grace, achieve a certain success in conquering their unruly passions and their blindly driven desires. This would result in a state of inner peace, a tranquillity in the soul where the violent demands of passion are subdued. They referred to this resultant state of peace by the Greek word "apatheia." It meant literally a state without passion, a quiet in the soul.

They understood that to foster the growth of the Holy Spirit's gift of Fortitude and achieve this state of peace and calm in the soul they had to do their part. They developed what they called the practice of "asceticism." This concept comes from another Greek word, "askesis." It means discipline, especially the discipline of a soldier training in preparation for a battle or the discipline of an athlete in training for competition in sports events. As part of their asceticism, both soldiers before battle and athletes before their sports competitions traditionally rubbed or "anointed" themselves with oil for greater agility.

The Christian soldier and athlete are, in a spiritual sense, likewise "anointed" by the Holy Spirit in preparation to win the crown of victory from Christ. Indeed, St. Paul used these images of the soldier and the athlete extensively in his own writings. He understood military life because the famed Roman legions were everywhere in his day. As a native of Tarsus in Asia Minor (modern Turkey) and as a result of his missionary journeys to so many ancient Greek cities, he was also familiar with the Greek Olympic games. In his Second Letter to Timothy, St. Paul used the imagery of military and athletic discipline to describe both his own personal asceticism and that of young Timothy. He sums up his own present situation in these words:

> I for my part am already being poured out like a libation. The
> time of my dissolution is near. I have fought the good fight, I

have finished the race, I have kept the faith. From now on a merited crown awaits me; on that Day the Lord, just judge that He is, will award it to me. (2 Timothy 4:6-8)

Just as St. Paul gained many good insights into the spiritual life from the world of sports, we, too, can do the same. A contemporary sports legend, Vince Lombardi, is often quoted as saying, "Winning isn't the main thing, it's the only thing!" Perhaps he was in some respects echoing a teaching of St. Paul. In his first letter to his Greek converts at Corinth, who would certainly have known and loved the ancient Olympic games, St. Paul wrote on this very theme:

You know that while all the runners in the stadium take part in the race, the award goes to one man. In that case, run so as to win! Athletes deny themselves all sorts of things. They do this to win a crown of leaves that withers, but we a crown that is imperishable.
I do not run like a man who loses sight of the finish line. I do not fight as if I were shadowboxing. What I do is discipline my own body and master it, for fear that after having preached to others I myself should be rejected. (1 Corinthians 9:24-27)

The competitiveness inherent in the athlete is a good symbol of the Christian striving to win the crown of life. Two brief reflections from the sports world illustrate this point. First, athletes know instinctively that anything worth achieving, any medal or competition worth winning, takes the sacrifice and hard work of discipline, training, and workouts. These wear and tear on the athlete, even to the point of suffering. As a popular saying among athletes reminds us: "No pain, no gain!"

The Holy Spirit convinces us of the same value in our striving for our spiritual goals. Without sacrifice, self-denial, and effort, we will never advance very far in the development of our Christian lives. At the same time, the Holy Spirit reminds us by His inspirations that no sacrifice or effort is possible without Fortitude, a gift He alone gives us.

WE NEED THE SPIRIT'S COURAGE TO
ANSWER THE CALL TO "TOTAL CONVERSION"

For anyone who wants to take the spiritual life seriously, there is only one true Christian response found in the Gospel. It is the readiness to give up everything to attain Christ. We have discovered the treasure hidden in the field, we have found the pearl of great price. Now we must go and sell all that we have to make that field and that pearl our own (cf. Matthew 13:44-46).

The Example of St. Francis

We have an example of this generous response in the life of St. Francis. Even though he was only at the beginning of his own conversion process, he was convinced of the need to sacrifice anything it would take to follow Jesus faithfully. This conviction came to him after the Lord in a dream had called him to discipleship. This happened near the little town of Spoleto, Italy. St. Bonaventure described Francis' immediate reaction:

> In the morning Francis went back to Assisi without delay. He was overjoyed and had no care for the future; he was already a model of obedience and he waited patiently on God's Will. He withdrew from the busy life of his trade and begged God in His goodness to show him what he should do. He prayed constantly until he was consumed with a passionate longing for God and was ready to give up the whole world in his desire for his heavenly home and think nothing of it. He realized that he had discovered the treasure hidden in the field and like the wise trader in the Gospel he could think of nothing but how he might sell all he had and buy the pearl he had found. He still did not know how to go about it, but at the same time he was forced to conclude that a spiritual venture could only begin by rejecting the world and that victory over himself would mark the beginning of his service of Christ. (*Major Life*, Chapter I, Par. 4)

St. Francis truly possessed great generosity for making sacrifices, inspired in him by the promptings and encouragement of the Holy Spirit!

A second thought again comes from a saying of Vince Lombardi. As a great football coach, he had the ability to motivate his football players to play their hearts out. This was especially true when the competition was the toughest. He would inspire his players with a saying he made famous: "When the going gets tough, the tough get going!" In His own unseen way, the Holy Spirit motivates us, and moves our hearts to accomplish great things or endure against extreme odds for the sake of the Kingdom of Heaven. When the going gets tough, the Spirit of Courage gets us going!

Confirmation Gives Us the Strength of the Holy Spirit

This courage and discipline forms our personal asceticism. This idea made its way even into the ancient rite of the Sacrament of Confirmation. Our traditional understanding has always been that in Confirmation we receive a renewed outpouring of the Holy Spirit that makes us soldiers of Christ. As set forth earlier, soldiers in ancient times anointed themselves for greater agility in battle since they fought in hand-to-hand combat. The Christians likewise viewed their anointing in the Sacrament of Confirmation as an anointing to carry on their spiritual warfare.

It is helpful to recall the fact that the conferring of the Holy Spirit in Confirmation is signified by a two-fold sign. First, there is the imposition of hands by the Bishop. This signifies that he is communicating the Spirit from himself to the one being confirmed. Second, there is an anointing of the person with the oil of chrism. This signifies that the new soldier of Christ is being readied for battle; the new athlete of Christ is being readied to compete to win the imperishable crown of life.

Related to the Confirmation rite was a traditional symbolic ceremony. It expressed the courage and strength one needed to defend his or her faith now as an adult Christian and soldier of

Christ. After confirming the person, the Bishop gave them a gentle slap on the cheek. It was a reminder of the readiness he or she would need in order to endure the suffering for his or her Faith in times of persecution.

This ceremony reminds me of a humorous incident that was told to me some years ago by a former prison chaplain. He had once prepared a number of prisoners to receive the Sacrament of Confirmation. When the Bishop arrived, he was going to question the prisoners to see how well they understood their Faith. The chaplain said to him, "Bishop, don't bother. I only taught the prisoners two things." The Bishop, somewhat startled, said, "Oh, what did you teach them?" The chaplain answered, "The first thing I taught them was how to make the Sign of the Cross. And the second thing I taught them was that when you slap them, not to slap you back."

THE IMPORTANCE OF "SPIRITUAL WARFARE"

In contemporary spirituality, we have probably moved too far away from the notion of "spiritual combat" or struggle. As a result, many Catholics today have the rather common but mistaken notion that holiness is easy. I once had thought of writing a book entitled *Getting To Heaven On a Credit Card*. When a person has a credit card, he or she can easily feel like spending in a carefree manner. But this feeling will probably disappear when the first financial statement arrives. Only then does one realize what he or she must pay!

It is the same in the spiritual life! As Sirach soberly reminds us:

When you come to serve the Lord, prepare yourself for trials. Be sincere of heart and steadfast, undisturbed in time of adversity. Cling to Him, forsake Him not; thus will your future be great. Accept whatever befalls you, in crushing misfortune be patient; for in fire gold is tested, and worthy men in the crucible of humiliation. (Sirach 2:1-5)

Our Lord Himself illustrated this notion of spiritual warfare in

His parable of the sower and the seed (Matthew 13:4-23). He tells us that part of the seed fell on rocky ground where it had little soil. It sprouted at once because the soil had no depth. But then the sun rose and scorched it; the sprout began to wither for lack of roots. A few verses later, Jesus explains what this symbolizes:

> The seed that fell on patches of rock is the man who hears the message and at first receives it with joy. But he has no roots, so he lasts only for a time. When some setback or persecution involving the message occurs, he soon falters. (Matthew 13:20-21)

The point Our Lord is making here is that if we want to follow Him with perseverance to the end of our spiritual journey, we have to be willing and ready to endure struggles and make sacrifices, and not simply expect to enjoy His blessings and consolations. Many who begin to follow Jesus give up at the first indication of sacrifice and self-denial. They mistakenly thought it would all be one big beautiful rose garden! But they never saw the thorns! Realistically, we must be ready to do whatever it takes to serve the Lord faithfully. After all, along with the sunshine in life, there is always a little rain from time to time!

Christian Courage in Fighting the Good Fight

In the Liturgy of the Hours, we find an inspiring responsory for the feast of St. Charles Lwanga and his companions. They were the martyrs of Uganda, canonized by Pope Paul VI. This responsory sums up the deep meaning of Christian courage in fighting the good fight:

> We are warriors now, fighting on the battlefield of faith, and God sees all we do; the angels watch and so does Christ. What honor and glory and joy to do battle in the presence of God, and to have Christ approve our victory. Let us arm ourselves in full strength and prepare ourselves for the ultimate struggle with blameless hearts, true faith and unyielding courage.

The Holy Spirit Strengthens Us in the Struggles of Life

May the Holy Spirit inspire and motivate us also with a similar courage!

Footnotes

1. Interestingly, when Our Lord begins His preaching in His own hometown at Nazareth, He Himself refers to a passage in Isaiah (61:1-2) about His being "anointed" by the Spirit. He did this in order to explain His true identity and the purpose of His mission.

   He came to Nazareth where He had been reared, and entering the synagogue on the Sabbath as He was in the habit of doing, He stood up to do the reading. When the book of the prophet Isaiah was handed to Him, He unrolled the scroll and found the passage where it was written: "The spirit of the Lord is upon Me; therefore He has anointed Me. He has sent Me to bring glad tidings to the poor, to proclaim liberty to captives, recovery of sight to the blind and release to prisoners, to announce a year of favor from the Lord." Rolling up the scroll He gave it back to the assistant and sat down. All in the synagogue had their eyes fixed on Him. Then He began by saying to them: "Today this Scripture passage is fulfilled in your hearing." (Luke 4:16-21)

2. As the Second Divine Person, Our Lord already possessed a fullness of unity with the Holy Spirit, the Third Divine Person. The visible descent of the Holy Spirit in the form of a dove upon Jesus in His humanity was meant to be a visible anointing for others to see. It would serve as a sign that Jesus truly possessed a fullness of the Holy Spirit, Whom He would later be able to give to others.

Chapter 10

The Holy Spirit's Gift of Fortitude

S T. PAUL TEACHES US THAT the Holy Spirit helps us in all our weaknesses (cf. Romans 8:26). How does the Holy Spirit do this? He gives us strength through the Gift of Fortitude or Courage.

FORTITUDE

St. Paul mentions the secret of this courage in a reminder he sent to his young co-worker, St. Timothy:

> For this reason, I remind you to stir into flame the Gift of God bestowed when my hands were laid on you. The Spirit God has given us is no cowardly spirit, but rather one that makes us strong, loving and wise. Therefore, never be ashamed of your testimony to Our Lord, nor of me, a prisoner for His sake; but with the strength which comes from God bear your share of the hardship which the Gospel entails. (2 Timothy 1:6-8)

St. Bonaventure wrote that Fortitude is a special inpouring of divine love that is communicated to our will, and it gives our will the impulse and energy to do great things joyfully and fearlessly. Fortitude strengthens us and enables us to overcome difficulties and obstacles of all kinds. Some are the difficulties we experience in our own personal growth in holiness. These arise from our attempts to come closer to God. Other difficulties are those we encounter in trying to carry out our ministry in the Church.

Fortitude helps us to persevere in the service of God in spite of every obstacle. The gift of Fortitude brings with it determination, assurance, joy, and a hope of some success. It also assists us with courage, a courage to do three things. First, Fortitude helps us to resist temptations steadfastly and unwaveringly. Despite the attraction temptations have to our human weakness, we can learn to resist them with firm determination. Second, Fortitude gives us the courage to renounce the world's empty promises and its allurement of riches, honors, and popularity. We come to see the vanity of the world, the fleeting brevity of the pleasures of the flesh, and the shallowness of the pride of our own ego. By Fortitude we are empowered to reject these evils for the sake of Christ and His love. Third, Fortitude gives us the courage to bear hardships and persecutions with patience as well as with a sense of hope, and even with joy!

Fortitude and Courage

Though we use the words "fortitude" and "courage" interchangeably, they actually have slightly different meanings. Fortitude comes from the Latin "fortis" — "strong." It means the moral strength or patient endurance to bear with afflictions, privations, or temptations. It is the passive strength to resist an attack, as defending a fort under siege. It is the strength needed to endure a long and painful illness, or persecution, and even martyrdom. Fortitude may be needed simply to remain faithful to one's own moral principles or to fulfill one's responsibilities and vocational commitments in life.

Courage, on the other hand, comes from the Latin "cor" — "the heart." Courage is a quality of mind and heart that enables us to encounter difficulties and dangers with firmness or without fear. It implies a sense of bravery. Its opposite, discouragement, means to lose heart, to be overwhelmed by fear or dread of impending difficulty. Courage is a more active strength, moving a person to undertake difficult or dangerous tasks. Unlike fortitude which is more on the "defense," resisting assault, courage goes more on the "offense," correcting injustice or attacking other evils. In the language of the sports world, fortitude is the virtue of a strong defense, and courage is the virtue of a strong offense!

It is very helpful to keep these two aspects of fortitude in mind. As a result, we can distinguish two kinds of actions that the Gift of Fortitude helps us to accomplish. The first is "doing" (to do). This is courage. Without hesitation or fear it moves us to undertake arduous tasks, such as accomplishing tireless activity, overcoming dangers and weariness, carrying out great undertakings, and ignoring human respect. The second kind of action is "enduring" (to endure). This is fortitude. It gives us the strength to hold firm in difficulties of all sorts, not to surrender or give up in the face of hardship or opposition.

THE NEED FOR THE SPIRIT OF COURAGE

The spiritual life is certainly not for the faint-hearted. It demands courage, and that courage must come from the Holy Spirit. Following the spiritual life is like running an obstacle course; there are difficulties to overcome all along the way.

Some of these difficulties come from within us, such as our own fears, our own inadequacies and limitations, even our own passions. Some of them come from outside of us, such as any opposition or persecution that we may encounter, any misunderstanding or rejection from others that we might experience, or any discouragement in the face of overwhelming tasks with seemingly inadequate resources.

The Apostles' Need for the Spirit of Courage

These were the same difficulties the Apostles faced as Jesus left them at the time of His Ascension. As we have already seen, He had made them His witnesses. They were to give witness to Him not only in Jerusalem, in Judea, and in Samaria, but yes, even to the very ends of the earth (cf. Acts 1:8). Our Lord knew the opposition that would come from those who refused to believe, as well as the persecutions that awaited the Apostles. He knew, for example, the hardships they would encounter —inadequate food, rest, or clothing. He also foresaw the dangers from wild animals, floods, and famine. He understood the fatigue of traveling — there were certainly no modern conveniences of travel in those days. He likewise knew the discouragement that would come from the lack of results and from the rejection on the part of so many. No wonder Our Lord told the Apostles to wait in Jerusalem to receive the power of the Holy Spirit (cf. Acts 1:4-5, 8).

The coming of the Holy Spirit on Pentecost transformed the Apostles profoundly, from fearful men to fearless disciples. They no longer felt the need to stay behind the locked doors of the Upper Room. Instead, they went out to the crowd and began to proclaim the Gospel message boldly (Acts 2:4).

The Apostles were not even intimidated by threats. For example, the Apostles Peter and John, when put on trial, stood confidently before the Sanhedrin (cf. Acts 3-4). Many of these Jewish leaders were trying to forbid them to preach in the Name of Jesus again. St. Peter's display of confidence is even more remarkable in the light of the fact that when he had been questioned on Holy Thursday night by a young servant girl about his being a disciple of Jesus, he ended up denying Him three times! (Matthew 26:69-70).

Our Need for the Spirit's Courage

It can be very difficult at times to speak the truth when we feel a person will dislike us as a result of it. Someone may scorn and ridicule us for what we have to say, or become angry with us when we take an unpopular stand, especially on a moral issue. We feel the pressure to "conform" and simply go along with the crowd.

As a result, we may be gravely tempted to water down our convictions or to compromise our beliefs. We may even be tempted to mask our true feelings and keep quiet altogether. This can lead to an old sin called "human respect." It has nothing to do with Christian respect and reverence for the God-given dignity of each person. That would be a virtue, an expression of charity toward our neighbor. Rather, "human respect" proceeds from our timidity or fear of what others may think or say about us. This could easily lead us to compromise our basic moral principles or even to deny or distort the truth.

The Pressure of "Human Respect"

In his Gospel St. John cites a striking example of this "human respect." At one point he presents a summary of the reactions of many of the Jewish leaders in the Sanhedrin as well as of others to Our Lord and His message:

> There were many, even among the Sanhedrin, who believed in Him; but they refused to admit it because of the Pharisees, for fear they might be ejected from the synagogue. They preferred the praise of men to the glory of God. (John 12:42-43)

Was not Pontius Pilate also guilty of the sin of human respect? Throughout the trial of Jesus, Pilate repeatedly asserted that he personally found Our Lord innocent of all charges. He likewise knew that it was only out of jealousy that the chief priests had handed Jesus over to him (Mark 15:10). Yet, he gave in to the loud shouts and demands of the crowd to win their favor. He perpetrated such an injustice that he released a known murderer and crucified the Lord of Life:

> So Pilate, who wished to satisfy the crowd, released Barabbas to them; and after he had had Jesus scourged, he handed Him over to be crucified. (Mark 15:15)

As in Pilate's case, this temptation to "human respect" can be especially difficult for Catholics in public life (for example, in politics, show business, or professional sports). Catholics often feel the pressure to compromise their religious beliefs and moral values for the sake of seeming to preserve their popularity. After all, society views it as essential today to be "politically correct." If Catholics lack the courage to meet the challenge of the moment (and it can certainly be a difficult trial for any one of us!) to say what they believe and believe what they say — it may seem easier to accept a compromised position. In such a case, a Catholic may claim to be "personally opposed" to some morally wrong course of action (for example, abortion or sexual perversion), but at the same time claim that he or she cannot do anything to correct the moral wrong. The individual may attempt to justify his or her action by arguing: "I can't impose my morality on others."

This temptation to "human respect" runs the risk of denying Our Lord. Dire consequences, such as the weakening of our faith, or the continuance of injustice and immorality or the like, would certainly follow. In contrast, it could be a tremendous occasion to acknowledge the Lord publicly and win His blessing:

> Whoever acknowledges Me before men I will acknowledge before My Father in Heaven. Whoever disowns Me before men I will disown before My Father in Heaven. (Matthew 10:32-33)

We should often pray for people in public life whose example and values influence and inspire many others. After all, we can never really be sure how we might act if put to the same test. For ourselves, the admonition of Our Lord certainly applies:

> Be on guard, and pray that you may not undergo the test. The spirit is willing but nature is weak. (Matthew 26:41)

The Apostles Display Great Courage

In the example cited above involving the Apostles Peter and John (Acts 4:5-22), both of them were strengthened with courage from the Holy Spirit.

> Then Peter, filled with the Holy Spirit, spoke up . . . (Acts 4:8).

They defended their faith in Jesus with a remarkable degree of calm and confidence. They rejected all "human respect." They were determined to be faithful to Jesus, their Lord and God, and to His command to them to go forth and preach the Gospel to every person at any cost:

> Observing the self-assurance of Peter and John, and realizing that the speakers were uneducated men of no standing, the questioners were amazed. Then they recognized these men as having been with Jesus... They made it clear (to Peter and John) that under no circumstances were they to speak the name of Jesus or teach about Him. Peter and John answered: "Judge for yourselves whether it is right in God's sight for us to obey you rather than God. Surely we cannot help speaking of what we have heard and seen." At that point they were dismissed with further warnings... They were filled with the Holy Spirit and continued to speak God's word with confidence. (Acts 4:13, 18-21, 31)

Furthermore, the Apostles became even willing to suffer joyfully for the Lord. In fact, they were scourged for continuing to preach about Jesus:

> The Sanhedrin called in the Apostles and had them whipped. They ordered them not to speak again about the name of Jesus, and afterward dismissed them. The Apostles for their part left the Sanhedrin full of joy that they had been judged worthy of ill treatment for the sake of the Name. Day after day, both in the Temple and at home, they never stopped teaching and proclaiming the Good News of Jesus the Messiah. (Acts 5:40-42)

We can see from these experiences of the Apostles, which occurred shortly after Pentecost, that the Holy Spirit had brought about a profound change in them. All their fear had been driven out; ardent love now motivated them. With the Holy Spirit's help, they possessed the courage to conquer all obstacles. With the Holy Spirit's help, we, too, can overcome all obstacles. As a retreat director once said, "No matter what difficulties you face, if God is with you, you are always in the majority!" The Holy Spirit is our majority!

Chapter 11

Patience: A Virtue Flowing From Fortitude

SOME FRUITS OF THE SPIRIT OF COURAGE

W HEN THE HOLY SPIRIT is present in us, His actions produce good effects in our lives. One such good effect is the practice of the virtue of Patience. The Holy Spirit's Gift of Fortitude helps patience to grow.

PATIENCE

Patience is certainly one of the most pervasive of Christian virtues simply because we need it in so many areas of our daily lives. Three such areas we shall consider are patience with ourselves, with others, and with the events of everyday living.

Patience with One's Self

We need a great deal of patience, first with ourselves. For many people, this is the most difficult of all areas of patience. Certainly, many reasons account for this. I would like to focus basically on one of them. Many people today have what is called a "poor self-image." This results in low self-esteem. They often fail to see the good within themselves. They tend to view themselves in negative terms. They put down their own potential for good, or they judge themselves to be quite inadequate and incompetent.

A low self-esteem often traces back to a person's early childhood. If the child did not receive sufficient affirmation or positive encouragement, his or her sense of confidence and security may have failed to develop adequately. Furthermore, if unrealistically high expectations were placed on the child by parents or others, the child would have inevitably fallen short of them. If the child was then criticized for not achieving demanding goals, or for "making mistakes," this would only have further eroded his or her self-esteem and self-image. All the child's efforts, even the best, would come to mean nothing. This could easily result in the child becoming shy and lacking in self-confidence, because of the feeling of being "incapable" of doing anything right.

This attitude, in turn, often leads the child to the feeling of being "unlovable." Such children instinctively feel that nobody would want to love them or be their friend, if that person only knew how they could not do even the simplest things correctly. They become hesitant to try again in the future for fear of making new mistakes for which they again might be corrected or criticized. Such children often experience, and usually continue to experience through adulthood, a difficult time accepting themselves for who they truly are. The final result adds up to what we call a "poor self-image."

Dealing patiently with a poor self-image

I believe most people experience something of this difficulty in their lives. Now if this negative attitude toward one's self is very strong, a person may well have feelings of rejecting himself or herself (at least insofar as their self-image is seen to be "negative" or inadequate). At times, however, this may actually produce a reaction in the opposite direction, resulting in what we call a "perfectionist." Certain people who reject a negative self-image of being incompetent or incapable end up trying to prove their self-worth by what they do. They feel that if they could only accomplish certain tasks (usually very "significant" tasks!) or achieve certain goals (and they must be "outstanding" goals!) they would thereby "prove" their own self-worth.

Actually, this is really frustrating and self-defeating. The reason is simple: one's self-worth is not something one can "prove"; it is rather something one must "accept." One's human dignity or self-worth is a "given" in life, not something that must be proven.

One's real worth as a human person lies in what one is — ultimately, in his or her dignity as a child of God, created in His image and likeness. One's worth does not depend on what one achieves or on one's ability to be a productive contributor. At the same time, one's God-given human dignity is not lost by disabilities or sufferings of any kind. Terence Cardinal Cooke suffered for over ten years with painful cancer before he died. No one knew of his sufferings because he kept them hidden from others while he carried on his important task of directing the Archdiocese of New York, one of the largest and most demanding in the world. Shortly before his death he wrote:

> Life is no less beautiful when it is accompanied by illness or weakness, hunger or poverty, physical or mental disease, loneliness or old age.

Perfectionists instinctively assume that they will win the esteem and approval of others by always doing everything perfectly. This also becomes the basis for their own self-esteem. At the same time, they create for themselves a "good" self-image. It is no wonder, however, that such persons often grow up very sensitive about making any mistakes. The reason is simple. If perfectionists made any mistakes, then they would no longer be "perfect." They would feel that others would no longer accept them, and they would have a hard time accepting themselves. These mistakes would shatter the fragile basis of their own self-worth and "good" self-image. Carried over into the spiritual life this could even mean that, if they sinned or made other mistakes in their lives, God Himself would not love them any more because He would no longer see them as "perfect."

We all need a good deal of patience to accept the fact that we are not perfect, that we can and do make mistakes. In the spiritual life this also means that we can and do sin. This opens the way to humility, which is simply the truth about ourselves. This in turn becomes the basis for both the freedom and the ability necessary to become more fully who we really are. We need patience with ourselves to do this. All real growth, whether physical, emotional or spiritual, takes time. Some people cannot wait. They want to rush the whole process, like the person who prayed, "God, give me patience, but give it to me right away." It takes a long time to overcome our sins and break our sinful attachments. We can only acquire patience by learning to be a little more realistic about ourselves every day.

It reminds me of a situation of a young lady I met when I drove through a toll booth at a parking lot. She seemed to be new at her job as a parking attendant. Probably figuring she was going to make a lot of mistakes, she wanted people to know that fact ahead of time. So, she had hung a poster outside her toll booth window that read, "Don't be upset with me, God isn't finished with me yet." As long as the Holy Spirit is at work in us with His gifts and fruits, we are not yet finished either!

There is a humorous story dealing with the "perfectionist" attitude that involves St. Francis de Sales. He was a very kind bishop known for his gentleness and common sense. One time he was sent to a cloistered convent to make a visitation of the community there. In the course of speaking privately with one of the elderly nuns, she burst out into tears in front of him. With solicitude the saint asked the nun what was wrong. She answered, "I have been a nun now for over fifty years, and I'm not perfect yet!" Calmly reassuring her, the saint answered, "Sister, if you become perfect five minutes before you die, that will be soon enough!"

What a relief such an attitude is in the face of any driven anxiety to be "perfect" all at once. How much more relieved we will all feel when we can accept this fact for ourselves. At the same time I am sure many "Alleluias" will be sung to God in thanksgiving by those who have had to live with us until we finally realized this!

Patience With Others

The second kind of patience we need is patience with others. The faults and shortcomings of others can hit us right between the eyes. Many times our neighbor's faults are very real and objective. Sometimes, however, we can exaggerate them and in fact, in a few instances — especially with people with whom we may have had long-standing difficulties — we can even perceive faults which actually do not exist. (Remember, not only can beauty be in the eyes of the beholder, but even the lack of it as well!) When we become upset with others we can easily become judgmental of them in our thoughts, critical of them in our words, annoyed at them in our attitudes, and angry at them in our actions.

Impatience, anger, and annoyance can wreak havoc in our spiritual lives. Each can prove to be a big obstacle that hinders our growth in our relationship to God and to our neighbor. The Holy Spirit will reproach our conscience for these attitudes. St. Paul warns:

> Never let evil talk pass your lips; say only the good things men need to hear, things that will really help them. Do nothing to sadden the Holy Spirit with whom you were sealed against the day of redemption. Get rid of all bitterness, all passion and anger, harsh words, slander, and malice of every kind. In place of these, be kind to one another, compassionate and mutually forgiving, just as God has forgiven you in Christ. (Ephesians 4:29-32)

St. Francis taught his friars this same point in his Rule of 1223. In Chapter 7, he wrote about the type of penance that was to be imposed by the friars in authority on any friar who sinned. He stated that those in authority "must be careful not to be angry or upset if a friar has fallen into sin, because anger or annoyance in themselves

131

or in others makes it difficult to be charitable." If the person in authority were to remain angry and annoyed, it certainly would make it difficult — at times almost impossible — for the erring person to come forward and seek forgiveness and reconciliation.

Patience and the control of anger

As we experience anger and annoyance, we need courage and self-discipline to bring these feelings under control. If we do not control them, they will end up controlling us. This is part of the self-discipline or "asceticism" needed in our spiritual life. It leads to the calming and conquering of our passions.

As stated previously, the early Christians referred to this calming of the passions by the Greek word "apatheia" (literally, without passion). Apatheia is a state of tranquillity that arises within our soul after we have basically subdued the unruly movements of our passions. This should not be confused with a temporary feeling of tranquillity that could result simply from having no difficulties or disturbances for a period of time. This can happen if things are going well or if we are dealing with pleasant people. In such cases, we might be tempted to think that we have acquired a high degree of the virtue of patience, and that we have gotten rid of all our impatience. But such circumstances are not the true norm by which to judge our patience. As St. Francis wrote in one of his admonitions:

> We can never tell how patient or humble a servant of God is when everything is going well with him. But when those who should cooperate with him do the exact opposite then we can tell. A man has as much patience and humility as he has then and no more. (Admonition 13)

Patience is an aspect of charity. St. Paul lists patience as the first quality of true charity: "Love is patient" (1 Corinthians 13:4). Through prayer and effort we can acquire this important fruit of the Holy Spirit.

Patience is absolutely necessary in our lives as Christians. It is the basis of unity in our families, religious communities, parishes, and areas of work or recreation. Patience operates like the rubbing of two diamonds together. Because it is a very hard stone, one diamond must rub up against another diamond in order to wear away the rough edges and to bring out the beauty in each diamond. A similar thing happens with us. The rough edges of our characters — our self-centeredness, impulsiveness, obstinacy, and the like — rub against one another and eventually get worn away by the work of the Holy Spirit. St. Francis de Sales said it well: "It is a great part of our perfection to learn to bear with one another in our imperfection." Our bearing with one another is the very goal of our patience.

Patience and growth in holiness

How does patience help us grow in holiness? The faults and shortcomings of our neighbors provoke in us feelings of discomfort, inconvenience, annoyance, and at times even intense anger. These feelings rise up inside us because of our reactions to the irritating words or actions or attitudes of others. This aspect can be seen very clearly in regard to the most difficult of all forms of patience, namely, the patience connected with loving our "enemies." Our Lord taught the necessity of this kind of love in His Sermon on the Mount:

> You have heard the commandment: "You shall love your countryman but hate your enemy." My command to you is: love your enemies, pray for your persecutors. This will prove that you are sons of your heavenly Father, for His sun rises on the bad and the good, He rains on the just and the unjust. If you love those who love you, what merit is there in that? Do not tax collectors do as much? And if you greet your brothers only, what is so praiseworthy about that? Do not pagans do as much? In a word, you must be perfect as your heavenly Father is perfect. (Matthew 5:43-48)

Remember, by an "enemy" Jesus does not necessarily mean someone with a gun out to get us. We may actually never have that kind of an enemy during our whole lifetime. Rather, He means someone we find very difficult to love, or accept, or tolerate. Maybe the person has hurt us in some way. But whatever the reason may be — whether real, exaggerated or imaginary — that person has become very negative, maybe even hostile, to us. To deal with him or her will require a great deal of self-control on our parts! He or she will really test our patience, pushing us to our limit!

The root meaning of the word "patience" is from the Latin "patire" — to endure, put up with, bear with.[1] Patience enables us to endure what is either painful or inconvenient. As our emotions flare up in reaction to what we have to tolerate, our virtue consists in struggling, by the light and strength of the Holy Spirit, to check our raw emotional reaction and gradually gain the self-control necessary to deal with the person and the situation in an appropriately Christ-like manner.

By patience we learn to "respond" and not simply "react" to the persons or situations that annoy us. "Response" is reflective and proportionate; "reaction" is impulsive and often exaggerated. When we find it difficult to deal with a person, frequent prayer to the Holy Spirit for the grace of patience in our lives is the first step we should take.

Once we have prayed for the patience we need, then we must find the best ways to hold back a curt remark, or harsh annoyance, or an impulsive outburst. Many people say "count to ten"; that gives time to gain some measure of self-control and composure.

I once heard a humorous story about a saint (I believe it was St. Vincent Ferrer) who had to deal with a woman who told him she was constantly arguing with her husband. The saint said he had just the remedy for her. He told her that in the garden of the monastery there was a well filled with holy water. He gave her a jug full of it. He told her that whenever she felt she was going to have an argument with her husband, she should drink a full glass of the holy water and keep it in her mouth until she and her husband calmed down. Needless to say, the arguing soon stopped! After all, an argument takes two impatient people, not just one!

Patience With Daily Events of Life

A final area of patience is patience with the events and happenings of day-to-day life. Most people, I believe, would like to be able to control all their daily occurrences. We generally like to be in the driver's seat, to feel in control. But life is not like that. We do not have the control panel — God does! As an old popular song says: "He's got the whole world in His hands . . . He's got you and me, brother (sister), in His hands!"

How often we plan things one way and they end up quite another! We expect certain outcomes to happen, but they turn out much differently. How often we experience the truth of the saying, "Man proposes, but God disposes." And what God disposes may not always be to our liking.

This is where we need patience — in the face of disappointment or hardship or deprivation. Accepting God's Will in its dispositions for our lives may be a real test of the depth of our patience, of our ability to endure what may not be to our liking. Putting up with what we do not like can cause a great deal of frustration.

How we deal with that frustration is important. If we do not deal with it effectively, we may well end up with one of two undesirable possibilities. Sometimes it can build up until we "explode" (blow up outwardly) in an angry outburst. Now such an explosion has the potential of releasing a lot of pent up anger and frustration all at once. In certain instances this can actually lead people to a mutual resolution of problems or differences because the explosion makes one person aware of how deeply distressed the other person has been! In this situation, the anger can lead to a beneficial effect. However, this is frequently not the case. Such an explosion of anger usually leads to a further cleavage or separation between persons. In such situations, not only are the problems unresolved, but now they may have become even more difficult to resolve because of the added tension the anger creates.

At other times frustration can pile up until we "implode"

(collapse inwardly) into a deep depression. Frustration in the face of unresolved difficulties often produces anger within. Such frustration can get us down so badly that it deflates our feelings, frequently causing a mood of depression to come over us!

"Accepting" or "changing" the situation?

What attitude should we take toward frustrating situations? The popular "Serenity Prayer" offers one of the best approaches to start: "Lord, grant me the patience to accept the things I cannot change, the courage to change the things I can, and the wisdom to know the difference!"

When, despite our best efforts, we seem to be unable to do anything to change a situation or resolve it in any way, the best approach to find some serenity is to change our attitude toward it at least for the time being.

A humorous story illustrates this point well. A homeowner had crabgrass in his lawn. He tried all kinds of ways to get rid of it — uprooting it, spraying it, burning it, even changing the soil — but nothing worked. In his desperation, he wrote to the state agricultural department. He told of the numerous unsuccessful methods he had used to get rid of the weeds. Then he asked: "What would you suggest I do?" He got a letter back and it said: "We suggest you get to like crabgrass!"

To "accept a situation" does not mean we have to agree with it or like it. It also does not mean we will not have other opportunities to try again to change things. St. Monica, despite her prayers and best efforts, for a long time could not get her son, Augustine, to give up his sinful ways. She had to accept that fact for the present, but she did not have to agree with it. She had the courage to keep on praying for many more long years — sixteen in all — that things would change. Eventually they did, and we in the Church have all been the better for it for the past fifteen hundred years.

To "accept the situation" means to let go of anxious and useless worry over it. It is not to allow ourselves to lose all our peace of mind and heart over situations we cannot change anyway. Sometimes, especially with those people who tend to be "perfectionists," a situation that involves annoyance or even injustice becomes an "obsession," a driven thought that is never out of their mind day or night. Perfectionists can become so obsessed because the difficulty their mind focuses on has destroyed their "perfect" world.

An important part of learning to be patient is to begin by accepting the reality in which we live. When we cannot do anything about a situation, we have to learn to bear with it patiently. We have to learn to acknowledge the real situation that confronts us, rather than waste time and energy in all sorts of wishful thinking or needless worry.

Trusting in Divine Providence

In order to accept the reality we live in, we should learn to cultivate a deep trust in what we call "Divine Providence." This is the unceasing care God has for all of His creatures, especially for we human beings made in His image and likeness. By His Providence, God provides for all our needs. Our Lord sums this up in one of His most beautiful teachings from the Sermon on the Mount:

> I warn you then, do not worry about your livelihood, what you are to eat or drink or use for clothing. Is not life more than food? Is not the body more valuable than clothes? Look at the birds in the sky. They do not sow or reap, they gather nothing into barns; yet your Heavenly Father feeds them. Are not you more important than they? Which of you by worrying can add a moment to his life span? As for clothes, why be concerned? Learn a lesson from the way the wildflowers grow. They do not work, they do not spin, yet I assure you not even Solomon in all his splendor was arrayed like one of these. If God can clothe in such splendor the grass of the field which blooms today and is thrown on the fire tomorrow, will He not provide much more for you, O weak in faith! Stop worrying, then, over questions like, 'What are we to eat, or what are we to drink, or

what are we to wear?' The unbelievers are always running after these things. Your Heavenly Father knows all that you need. Seek first His kingship over you, His way of holiness, and all these things will be given you besides. Enough, then, of worrying about tomorrow. Let tomorrow take care of itself. Today has troubles enough of its own. (Matthew 6:25-34)

By this same Providence, God also directs all happenings both in nature and in human history to some greater good or benefit for us. This includes the events of our personal lives. We must share the conviction of St. Paul because it can greatly foster our sense of trust:

We know that God makes all things work together for the good of those who have been called according to His decree. (Romans 8:28)

This conviction is rooted in the fact that, despite appearances, the world's situation is still in God's hands. I remember while giving a retreat for college students, a young lady from Korea shared an incident that happened to her when she was a teenager living in her native country. She was on a crowded bus that was traveling down a rather steep, curving, mountainous road. The bus driver was driving quite fast. Everyone began to panic because they felt he was driving recklessly. She noticed a young boy fast asleep in the seat ahead of her. In her concern for him she woke him saying, "Aren't you afraid of how fast the driver is driving the bus?" "No," the little boy said, "I'm not afraid. The bus driver is my father." The little boy had complete confidence in his father.

God is our Father! We, too, must learn to trust Him even in our difficulties, for all things are in His loving and merciful hands. St. Francis de Sales gives us this inspiring reminder of the providential care of our Heavenly Father:

Do not look forward to what might happen tomorrow... The same everlasting Father Who cares for you today will take care of you tomorrow and every day. Either He will shield you from suffering, or He will give you unfailing strength to bear it. Be at peace then and put aside all anxious thoughts and imaginations.

To worry needlessly would mean we do not take this truth seriously in all its implications. It certainly pleases our Heavenly Father when we — like children approaching loving parents — approach Him with confidence.

Learning Even From Our Sins

We need to develop the conviction that God will draw good out of every situation if only we love and trust Him through it all. St. Augustine was convinced of this. To the words of St. Paul that God makes all things work together for good, he added the words: "Yes, even our sins!" We might ask, "What good can sin lead to?" Not that we want to commit sins deliberately, for sin is, of course, the greatest offense against God and in itself it causes the greatest harm to our spiritual lives. But if we have had the misfortune to sin, we must not give way to despair. Rather, we must remember that God can even then lead us to many spiritual insights that will aid our growth in the future. What are some of these insights?

Learning not to trust in our own strength

For example, from our falls into sin, we must realize that we cannot trust in our own virtue or strength. Rather, we should recognize our own personal moral weakness and our constant need for God's grace to do any good or overcome any evil. Our Lord very emphatically taught the need for the assistance of His grace to the Apostles at the Last Supper:

> Live on in Me, as I do in you. No more than a branch can bear fruit of itself apart from the vine, can you bear fruit apart from Me. I am the Vine, you are the branches. He who lives in Me and I in him, will produce abundantly, for apart from Me you can do nothing. A man who does not live in Me is like a

withered, rejected branch, picked up to be thrown in the fire and burnt. (John 15:4-6)

Did not St. Peter personally have to learn this lesson? At the same Last Supper, when Jesus foretold to all the Apostles they would leave Him, St. Peter protested he would not leave, saying he was ready to die for Jesus! Unfortunately, he was unaware that he was trusting in his own strength which would not be sufficient in time of trial. He had not yet realized both his own weakness and his need for God's grace. What happened? As is well known, he denied three times that he even knew Jesus! Afterward, however, he wept bitterly over his sin! He learned a very important lesson, but in a most painful way.

Learning not to condemn others

A second lesson we can learn from our own sins is not to condemn others when they sin. It would be hypocritical to condemn another person for their sins, while we ourselves are not free of our own sins. The Pharisees, who were so ready to stone the woman caught in adultery, had to learn this lesson painfully (cf. John 8:1-11). These men were quick to condemn the woman for her sin because they were no longer mindful of their own sins. Perhaps they had been repented of, or maybe they were simply denied by all kinds of excuses or by rationalizing them away. For whatever reason, their sins were forgotten.

When they asked Our Lord if the woman should be stoned to death for her sin of adultery, He challenged anyone among them who was without sin to condemn the woman by casting the first stone. Then Our Lord began to write in the sand with His finger. Whatever He wrote, it apparently indicated something to each of them that made them remember their own sins. This destroyed their self-righteous and condemning attitude. Leaving the woman uncondemned, they all dropped their stones and walked away.

This is a very important lesson for all of us. If we remember our need for forgiveness for our own sins, past and present and probably even future, we will be less ready to condemn anyone else. We can then receive the glorious promise of Our Lord:

> Do not judge, and you will not be judged. Do not condemn, and you will not be condemned. Pardon, and you shall be pardoned. Give, and it shall be given to you... For the measure you measure with will be measured back to you. (Luke 6:37-38)

Learning to be more grateful and loving

Finally, we can learn through our sins to be more grateful and loving to God for His infinite mercy without which we would have been lost because of our sins. It makes us realize the truth of Our Lord's words that one to whom more is forgiven loves more (cf. Luke 7:36-50). Deep gratitude for our sins being forgiven can be one of the strongest motives to love God intensely!

Footnotes

1. From a form of this same Latin verb also comes our English word, "passion" — literally, a suffering, a bearing with, an undergoing.

Chapter 12

Two Fruits of the Spirit of Courage: Faithfulness and Perseverance

T HE HOLY SPIRIT PRODUCES MANY of His fruits in us through His gift of Fortitude. Two fruits which especially depend on Courage are Faithfulness and Perseverance. Let us look closely at both of them.

FAITHFULNESS

St. Paul says that faithfulness or trustworthiness is the first quality we should have as servants of Christ:

> Men should regard us as servants of Christ and administrators of the mysteries of God. The first requirement of an administrator is that he prove trustworthy. (1 Corinthians 4:1-2)

The Qualities of Faithfulness

A sense of responsibility

Faithfulness includes a number of characteristics. It is first of all responsible. To be responsible means to feel an obligation for a certain task or office. Responsibility involves a sense of duty or commitment to a certain goal or undertaking, to see that it is accomplished as well as possible. Those who are responsible can be relied upon to give their best service to their appointed task.

If we are called, for example, to a ministry in the church, such as being a Eucharistic minister or a lector or a CCD teacher, do we fulfill our responsibilities regarding our particular ministry? Do we show up for the times we are appointed for ministry? If we must be absent, have we provided for a replacement to substitute for us so that the ministry does not suffer? If we are a Eucharistic minister, do we see to it, as far as we are charged to do so, that the hosts and wine to be used at the Mass are properly prepared? When we administer the Eucharistic Body and Blood of the Lord to others, do we do so with proper respect and reverence? When the Mass is over, do we see to it that the sacred vessels are properly purified? If we are lectors at Mass, do we review our liturgical readings beforehand? Or does neglect to do so lead to a less reverent and less effective proclamation of the Word of God? If we teach CCD, have we prepared our lessons adequately so that the young might be well-instructed in the truths of our Catholic Faith? Our sense of responsibility must not only be toward God, toward His greater honor and glory, but also toward our neighbors, who, as brothers and sisters in Christ, depend on our ministry to help them grow in their Faith.

A sense of loyalty

Another characteristic of faithfulness is loyalty. Loyalty is a pledge of undying faithfulness whether to our family or our Church or our country. To be loyal is to have a special honor and regard for those we hold in high esteem. To be loyal is to stand by those we are committed to in good times and in bad, in blessings and in difficulties. Perhaps at no time is loyalty more clearly exhibited than in times of struggle, opposition, and especially war. The proverbial friend in need is truly a loyal friend indeed!

At the time of the Revolutionary War for independence from Great Britain, an American patriot named Thomas Paine wrote an essay called *The Crisis*. He wrote it to arouse the colonists to take action and to fight for their freedom at any price. In the opening lines, Paine captures the meaning of loyalty in the young country's time of greatest need:

> These are the times that try men's souls. The summer soldier and the sunshine patriot will, in the crisis, shrink from the service of his country; but he that stands by it now, deserves the love and thanks of man and woman. Tyranny, like hell, is not easily conquered; yet we have this consolation with us, that the harder the conflict, the more glorious the triumph. What we obtain too cheap, we esteem too lightly; it is dearness only that gives everything its value.

These words can apply equally to the struggles of our spiritual warfare as they did to the American Revolution. By His grace, the Holy Spirit will sustain us so that we do not shrink back in times of crisis. It is easy to be a "summer soldier" and a "sunshine patriot," whether the cause is temporal or eternal. Just as warfare separates these surface patriots from the loyal ones, so the Cross distinguishes the summer and sunshine disciples from those who endure in wintry and overcast conditions. Loyalty perseveres and pays the dear price!

The greatest offense against loyalty is betrayal. Perhaps no one is held in greater shame than a traitor. A traitor is disloyal to his own, betraying the very confidence and trust others have put in him.

I was stationed for about ten years at a friary in Beacon, New York. This is a city located on the eastern shore of the Hudson River about ten miles north of and across the river from the famous military academy at West Point. Alongside the Hudson River, an historical sign marked a certain spot almost opposite the military academy. The sign commemorated a sad event in American history. It involved Benedict Arnold, the American officer who attempted to betray West Point into the hands of the British forces during the Revolutionary War. When his unsuccessful plot was uncovered, Arnold fled by this spot to a British frigate named the *Vulture* which lay at anchor on the Hudson River almost across from West Point. Arnold, banished from his own land as a traitor and equally despised even by the British for his act of treachery, died in England, a man without a country.

In our Faith, the name of Judas Iscariot is that of a traitor. He betrayed his Lord and Master for a price. He likewise betrayed the trust and confidence put in him by his call to be one of the twelve Apostles. He lacked the loyalty that marks every true follower of Jesus. It is the Holy Spirit Who will give us the grace to remain loyal until death, to choose the Lord above all things.

A sense of consistency

A third characteristic of faithfulness is consistency. Consistency is a very important quality in the spiritual life, as it is also in our daily life whether in our families or rectories or religious communities. For example, take consistency at prayer. If I pray only when I feel like praying, I will not get very far in my spiritual growth, any more than a parent who goes to work only when he or she feels like it will pay many of the family's bills. But if I learn to pray or at least try to, whether I feel like praying or not, then in spite of dryness or distractions or tiredness or listlessness, I would still make the effort to pray. Feeble as the effort may seem, I will have grown in faithfulness because I am learning to become more consistent in my spiritual life. And sooner or later, such consistency will pay off with good results!

There are a lot of things we do each day, not because we want to or feel like doing them, but because we know we must do them. A sense of duty, love, or compassion moves us to forget our own moods and preferences, and to make the effort required. I am sure many a parent with an infant child who is sick during the night does not "feel" like getting up to care for the tiny child, but love and a sense of responsibility motivate that parent.

Actually, our moods and feelings are least dependable for gauging spiritual growth; what we really need is a firm will and determination. St. Paul summed this point up when he wrote to his young disciple Timothy about the need to preach faithfully, no matter what his circumstances:

I charge you to preach the word, to stay with this task whether convenient or inconvenient — correcting, reproving, appealing, constantly teaching and never losing patience. For the time will come when people will not tolerate sound doctrine, but following their own desires will surround themselves with teachers who tickle their ears. They will stop listening to the truth and will wander off to fables. As for you, be steady and self possessed; put up with hardship, perform your work as an evangelist, fulfill your ministry. (2 Timothy 4:2-5)

What St. Paul writes about consistency in preaching, is a good norm for us, no matter what our responsibilities.

PERSEVERANCE

A second fruit of the Holy Spirit we shall consider here is perseverance. Perseverance is connected with patience and in a real sense builds upon it as a foundation. Perseverance deepens the level of endurance in our patience by allowing us to endure probably the hardest of all tests, the test of time. It is possible to bear with great pressures and tensions if we know they will soon end. But to know we have to endure them over a very long period of time or even for the rest of our lives usually proves to be the acid test! Striving to pray or spending time helping a homeless person for one year, for example, can be a treat. But to persevere at it for twenty-five or fifty years is no joke. It is bound at times to become almost an intolerable burden. Where will we get the strength to put up with it for so long? The Holy Spirit will give us His fruit of perseverance (sometimes also called "long-suffering").

The Importance of Perseverance

Our Lord knew the importance of perseverance. He tells us clearly in the Gospel:

> The man who holds out to the end is the one who will see
> salvation. (Matthew 24:13)

Perseverance produces many good effects in our spiritual life. It can serve to strengthen our love for God. In order to persevere our will has to remain fixed on God. It is with our willpower, constantly supported by God's grace, that we choose to love God. For the will to persevere, it must choose God again and again, in spite of all the changes of our circumstances, our mood swings, our "good days," and our "bad days." In the spiritual life, to quote an old airline commercial, we must "earn our wings" every day!

Perseverance also deepens our virtues. We acquire our virtues in the spiritual life by constant repetition. As the old saying goes, "Practice makes perfect." If we persevere daily in the practice of the virtues, they will soon become strong habits. Eventually, they will even become second nature to us!

On the other hand, if we do not persevere, our virtues will grow weak and ineffective. As a person who was once proficient in speaking a foreign language becomes quite "rusty" from lack of practice, so without perseverance we lose the ease and effectiveness of our virtues. This, in turn, will have negative consequences on our spiritual growth. As St. Augustine said many centuries ago: "If you are not going forward in the spiritual life, you are going backward. Not to advance is to decline."

The spiritual life might be compared to a marathon race. Many people begin in the contest, but not all end up crossing the finish line. Due to the long time and distance as well as the continuous and often grueling effort required, many drop out along the way. The same is true of the Christian life. To quote St. Augustine again: "Once the journey begins, the road becomes long." Perseverance is required to complete it. St. Paul shares his own experience in the imagery of a runner in a race:

> It is not that I have reached it yet, or have already finished my
> course, but I am racing to grasp the prize if possible, since I
> have been grasped by Christ (Jesus). Brothers, I do not think

of myself as having reached the finish line. I give no thought to what lies behind but push on to what is ahead. My entire attention is on the finish line as I run toward the prize to which God calls me — life on high in Christ Jesus. All of us who are spiritually mature must have this attitude. If you see it another way, God will clarify the difficulty for you. It is important that we continue on our course, no matter what stage we have reached. (Philippians 3:12-16)

St. Paul stresses here the importance of the need to persevere, to continue on the journey no matter what happens. Perseverance means growth and maturity. The traditional children's story of the tortoise and the hare reminds us of how much we can lose when we become complacent about whatever progress we feel we have already made. That is why St. Paul says he did not look back to the ground he had already covered; he only kept his eyes on the goal line, only on what distance still lay ahead of him to reach Christ Himself!

This is the imagery of the athlete straining forward to win. It reminds me of a remark once made by a professional football player. He was a wide receiver.[1] A sports reporter was interviewing him. He told the reporter: "I have never been caught directly from behind by a player on the opposite team." The reporter was surprised, and he asked, "How do you account for that, since you are not that fast and most of the defensive players on the other teams are quite fast?" The player answered: "After I catch that football, I don't break my stride. I keep my eyes fixed on the goal line, and I just keep saying to myself, 'I'm going to get there! I'm not going to let anyone stop me!'" I could just imagine St. Paul having the same determination.

The word "perseverance" is from the Latin, "per" — through, and "severus" — a difficult or severe thing. To persevere is to go through difficult times and trials. The trial of perseverance is ultimately the test of time. With the passage of time, burdens begin to feel heavier, our resolve begins to fade, boredom sets in, and all kinds of unforeseen opposition and stumbling blocks begin to show themselves. This is a test indeed! It is no wonder that in society today we often hear the expression: "Never say forever!" People today are frightened by the making of permanent commitments. They prefer a loose situation, flexible, nothing hard and fast, no binding obligations.

Yet, Christian life demands commitments that require perseverance. It is rooted in the very nature of love, because true love tends to endure forever. The vocations of Marriage or the Priesthood or the Religious life are of themselves life-long. They demand perseverance, especially through the trials that inevitably will arise regarding the pledge of commitment a person has made.

When Pope John Paul II visited the United States of America in 1979, I had the opportunity to attend his Mass for priests in Philadelphia. He said something in his homily that I believe I will never forget. "The God who heard you say 'Yes' does not now want to hear you say 'No.'" To remain faithful to our committed love, we need the Holy Spirit's fruit of perseverance. When the responsibilities and strains become burdensome, the Holy Spirit helps us to carry them; when our negative moods distress us, the Holy Spirit consoles us. Through Him we find the strength to keep on going and not give up. The Spirit of Life revives us, the Spirit of Truth enlightens us, and the Spirit of Courage sustains us!

Perseverance Fosters Spiritual Maturity

Another point about perseverance is that it plays a major role in the process of our maturing. If we give up on something at a stage when the going gets rough, we may never mature to the next stage of growth.

Take the stages of marriage for example. It is often said that a good marriage goes through three stages: (1) the Honeymoon, (2) the Disillusionment, (3) the Choice to Love. In the "Honeymoon" stage, everything is "super"; there's not a cloud in the sky. The newlyweds see each other through rose-colored glasses. He's my "Prince Charming," she's my "Beautiful Princess."

Then, "crash," reality hits! As a venerable old friar I used to be stationed with would say, "Love is blind, but marriage is the eye-opener!" Difficulties and tensions of all kinds arise. The strain between the couple may even seem to become overwhelming. "Is this the person I married?" This is the "Disillusionment" stage! Now they are looking at each other through very dark-colored glasses. This is when couples are tempted to give up, and many of them do.

Yet, they may actually be on the brink of a tremendous step toward maturing in their marital relationship. They can come to the third stage, the "Choice to Love." No longer do they see each other as the "perfect" person, being everything their partner expects them to be, as in the "Honeymoon" stage; nor are they totally "negative," without any redeeming qualities, as they might see each other in the "Disillusionment" stage. Now, they can look at each other without rose-colored or dark-colored glasses, but simply with clear glasses. They can see and accept each other as they really are — with their good qualities and bad, with their strengths and weaknesses. They can finally and honestly view each other as the persons they really are, not the persons they expected each other to be. Now each can freely choose the other as he or she really is. This is the maturing of the commitment of marriage. Perseverance has allowed them the time and opportunity for their own growth to take place so that they could finally make this genuine loving choice.

Perseverance Overcomes the Noonday Devil

One of the hardest aspects of the "test of time" is to deal with the sense of "listlessness" and "boredom" that frequently goes along with persevering at something. Doing the same task for years, caring for the same responsibilities, especially toward other people, can easily become routine, monotonous, and boring.

We get restless and want to break away from the situation. We look for something new and exciting, figuring that "variety is the spice of life." This certainly is a factor in the breaking of long range commitments in today's society, whether it be marriage, Priesthood, Religious life, even just living our Catholic Faith.

This is by no means a new problem. Even the desert "fathers" and "mothers"[2] of the 4th Century recognized the problem clearly. In ancient times, as we have seen, the desert was thought to be inhabited by demons. Through careful analysis of the ways they were tempted, these desert monks and nuns discerned various kinds of demons. They eventually came to identify eight different demons, each producing a different kind of temptation or "evil thought." The ultimate goal of these demons was, through these various evil thoughts or temptations, to seduce these holy men and women into sin or at least into discouragement so that they would abandon their lives of prayer and penance in the desert.

An early spiritual writer, Evagrius Ponticus (346-399) familiar with the spiritual teachings of the desert ascetics, seems to have been the first author to list the eight demons or evil thoughts: (1) gluttony, (2) lust, (3) avarice, (4) dejection, (5) anger, (6) listlessness, (7) vainglory, and (8) pride. Later, St. Gregory the Great (540-604) altered the list. He removed pride saying it belonged in a class all its own because it was the source and mother of all other vices. He then removed listlessness and in its place added envy. This revised list enumerated the famous seven capital or deadly sins: (1) vainglory, (2) envy, (3) anger, (4) dejection or (spiritual) sloth, (5) avarice, (6) gluttony, and (7) lust.

The demon or thought we are interested in is "dejection" or "listlessness." The desert dwellers called it "acedia" (or "accidie") from a Greek word meaning "not caring." It was a state of listlessness, a feeling of weariness and discontent resulting from a lack of interest. It was a general feeling of boredom. We can imagine how difficult this must have been in the desert. These holy men and women — worn down by fasting and prayer — lived lives of routine, in lonely cells in the desolate wilderness. No wonder the thought to get up and leave it all would enter their minds. This thought became one of the most feared of all the demons, and it was nicknamed the infamous "noonday devil" from a verse in one of the

Psalms which referred to the "devastating plague at noon" (Psalm 91:6).

It was a fact that most of the desert dwellers who quit their life of solitude, prayer and penance, did so at the noon of the day. This was when the heat was devastating, probably making many of them delirious and restless. Some abandoned their hermit form of religious life altogether, while many others, wandering restlessly from one hermitage or monastery to another, simply became vagabonds. They would stay for a while, and when they felt the restlessness again, they moved on.[3]

To persevere is to oppose the dreaded "noonday devil." To do this, we need the constant support of the Holy Spirit. He must help us find our consolation in His power to renew us. The Holy Spirit will lead us to Jesus Who will teach us how to find joy and fulfillment even in the ordinary things we do day after day, month after month, and year after year.

When I taught in a preparatory seminary, one of the seminarians had a clever poster. It read: "Jesus is the hum in the hum-drum!" When done out of love and for Jesus, even the most ordinary, prosaic tasks can be noble and fulfilling. No wonder St. Therese of Lisieux remarked: "To the thrill of ecstasy I prefer the monotony of sacrifice!"

St. Conrad of Parzham

One inspiring example of someone who persevered at simple things and turned them into stepping stones to great holiness is a Capuchin Franciscan, St. Conrad of Parzham (1818-1894). As a brother he was appointed to serve as porter at the shrine-friary of Our Lady of Altotting in Bavaria, Germany. He did this humble task for forty-three years during which he distinguished himself for very great charity, zeal, and patience. He always showed a special regard for the poor and destitute.

After his death, the Capuchin Order tried to present his case for canonization as a saint. However, the so-called "Devil's Advocate"[4] objected to Brother Conrad's canonization on the grounds that he had not done anything significant for the life of the Church. When feelings became intense between the Capuchin superiors and the Devil's Advocate, Pope Pius XI agreed to personally hear the arguments of both sides.

First, the Capuchins presented evidence of Brother Conrad's genuine holiness of life and zealous dedication as a religious. When it came his turn, the Devil's Advocate pleaded: "Your Holiness, how could you canonize this man? What good did he do of any significance for the life of the Church?" Pope Pius XI answered, "Father, if you took care of the door of a shrine for forty years and did not complain about it, I would canonize you!"

The Carmelite Martyrs of Compiégne

Not only does the Holy Spirit make us persevere through the test of monotony and routine, but He strengthens us to persevere in the face of great trials and persecution.

Let us look at a striking example of the Holy Spirit transforming a group of fearful people into a group of courageous martyrs. They are known as the martyrs of Compiégne. They were a group of sixteen Carmelite nuns who were guillotined during the French Revolution on July 17, 1794.

In August 1790, an anti-clerical revolutionary government then in power in France made all the nuns in the convent take an oath (called the oath of Liberté-Egalité) which strongly limited the Church's power. Afterwards, the nuns were forced to leave the convent at Compiégne and were dispersed into small groups throughout the town so that they could no longer live as a religious community. Dressing in secular garb, they nonetheless continued — albeit secretly — to live their religious lifestyle. A few years later, some local revolutionary followers accused the nuns of violating the law by living as religious, and then imprisoned sixteen of the original twenty-one nuns on June 22, 1794.

While in prison, the nuns retracted their oaths of loyalty to the government and began to practice once again all their usual religious exercises. This continued until July 12, when they were sent under police escort to Paris. While awaiting trial they continued to recite the Divine Office. Finally, on July 17 after a brief trial which was held without witnesses, the Carmelite nuns were sentenced to death. They were condemned as counter-revolutionaries and religious fanatics because they lived as religious under obedience to a superior, the prioress Mother Teresa of St. Augustine. Immediately after their trial, they went to the guillotine, chanting the "Miserere" (Psalm 51), the "Salve Regina" (the "Hail Holy Queen"), and the "Te Deum," a hymn of thanksgiving. When they finally reached the spot of execution (now called the "Place of the Nation"), the nuns knelt and called upon the help of the Holy Spirit, chanting the "Veni, Creator Spiritus." They then all renewed their baptismal promises and religious vows. As each nun — beginning with the youngest novice — mounted the scaffold, she obtained the blessing of the prioress; then, chanting God's praises and singing the "Salve Regina" she then ascended to the place of execution. It is said that during the executions an absolute silence prevailed.

In a play about the martyrs of Compiégne, called *The Dialogue of the Carmelites*, there is a dramatic scene at the end.[5] While the executions are taking place, the nuns are singing the "Salve Regina" in chorus. The "Salve Regina" gradually diminishes in volume as each nun is guillotined. When finally the prioress is about to be executed and the "Salve Regina" ceases, a woman pushes her way through the crowd. She was a nun who had left before the others were arrested. Her name in the play is Sister Blanche. As she arrives at the scaffold, she is not singing the "Salve Regina" but the final verses of the "Veni, Creator Spiritus." Thus, the Holy Spirit not only strengthened all the nuns to face death, but also helped Sr. Blanche to have the heroic courage to overcome her great fear and join her companions in bearing witness to Jesus' love. She met her death invoking the power of the Holy Spirit.

FAITHFULNESS AND PERSEVERANCE OPEN INTO ETERNITY

Faithfulness and perseverance are the special graces needed at the moment when Christ calls us from this life. In the Gospel, Jesus uses the image of a Master (Himself) Who delays in coming to call His servants (each of us). Our Lord tells us it will go well with each servant who is found ready and waiting when the Master knocks at the door and who opens the door immediately for Him to enter. This is especially so if the Master's return has been delayed. Jesus says:

> Be like men awaiting their Master's return from the wedding, so that when he arrives and knocks, you will open for him without delay. It will go well with those servants whom the Master finds wide awake on his return. I tell you, he will put on an apron, seat them at table, and proceed to wait on them. Should he happen to come at midnight or before sunrise and find them prepared, it will go well with them. (Luke 12:36-38)

Christ will serve us if we have served Him faithfully and perseveringly. He will tell us on the last day:

> Well done! You are an industrious and reliable servant. Since you were dependable in a small matter I will put you in charge of larger affairs. Come, share your Master's joy! (Matthew 25:21)

Let us then persevere in running the race and fighting the good fight, until we achieve the crown which God, in His love, has prepared for us. May we experience the Holy Spirit working in our lives until His work is brought to completion. We can apply to the Holy Spirit in a special way the inspiring words of Cardinal Newman:

> May He support us all the day long,
> Till the shades lengthen,
> And the evening comes,
> And the busy world is hushed,
> And the fever of life is over,
> And our work is done;

Then in His mercy may He give us:
A safe lodging,
And a holy rest,
And peace at the last.

Footnotes

1. These are the players who run down the field hoping to catch a long pass so as to gain many yards or even a touchdown.
2. These desert "fathers" and "mothers" were ascetical monks and nuns called "abbas" and "ammas" respectively.
3. Such monks became known as "gyrovagii" (literally, travelers moving in circles, those who make the rounds). These wandering monks were such a problem that when St. Benedict wrote his monastic rule in the 6th Century, he established as one of his vows the vow of stability, in order to prevent monks from moving endlessly from one monastery to the next.
4. The task of the "Devil's Advocate" is to find any and every possible reason why someone should not be canonized a saint.
5. From my own independent research, I could not substantiate all the details of this episode, but I presume the writer of the play based it on fact, as he did the rest of the play.